IMMIGRANT SCHOLARS IN RHETORIC, COMPOSITION, AND COMMUNICATION

NCTE Editorial Board: Steven Bickmore, Catherine Compton-Lilly, Deborah Dean, Antero Garcia, Bruce McComiskey, Jennifer Ochoa, Staci M. Perryman-Clark, Anne Elrod Whitney, Vivian Yenika-Agbaw, Kurt Austin, Chair, ex officio, Emily Kirkpatrick, ex officio

Immigrant Scholars in Rhetoric, Composition, and Communication

Memoirs of a First Generation

Edited by

LETIZIA GUGLIELMO
Kennesaw State University

SERGIO C. FIGUEIREDO
Kennesaw State University

National Council of Teachers of English
1111 W. Kenyon Road, Urbana, Illinois 61801-1096
www.ncte.org

Staff Editor: Bonny Graham
Interior Design: Jenny Jensen Greenleaf
Cover Design: Pat Mayer
Cover Image: iStock.com/Bluberries
NCTE Stock Number: 17392; eStock Number: 17408
ISBN 978-0-8141-1739-2; eISBN 978-0-8141-1740-8

©2019 by the National Council of Teachers of English.

All rights reserved. No part of this publication may be reproduced or transmitted in any form or by any means, electronic or mechanical, including photocopy, or any information storage and retrieval system, without permission from the copyright holder. Printed in the United States of America.

It is the policy of NCTE in its journals and other publications to provide a forum for the open discussion of ideas concerning the content and the teaching of English and the language arts. Publicity accorded to any particular point of view does not imply endorsement by the Executive Committee, the Board of Directors, or the membership at large, except in announcements of policy, where such endorsement is clearly specified.

NCTE provides equal employment opportunity (EEO) to all staff members and applicants for employment without regard to race, color, religion, sex, national origin, age, physical, mental or perceived handicap/disability, sexual orientation including gender identity or expression, ancestry, genetic information, marital status, military status, unfavorable discharge from military service, pregnancy, citizenship status, personal appearance, matriculation or political affiliation, or any other protected status under applicable federal, state, and local laws.

Every effort has been made to provide current URLs and email addresses, but because of the rapidly changing nature of the web, some sites and addresses may no longer be accessible.

Library of Congress Cataloging-in-Publication Data

Names: Guglielmo, Letizia, 1977- editor. | Figueiredo, Sergio C., editor.
Title: Immigrant scholars in rhetoric, composition, and communication : memoirs of a first generation / edited by Letizia Guglielmo, Kennesaw State University; Sergio C. Figueiredo, Kennesaw State University.
Description: Urbana, Illinois : National Council of Teachers of English, 2019.
  | Includes bibliographical references and index. | Summary: "Shares the experiences of first-generation immigrant scholars in rhetoric, composition, and communication and how those experiences shape individual academic identity and, in turn, the teaching of writing and rhetoric"—Provided by publisher.
Identifiers: LCCN 2019025845 (print) | LCCN 2019025846 (ebook) | ISBN 9780814117392 (trade paperback) | ISBN 9780814117408 (adobe pdf)
Subjects: LCSH: English language—Study and teaching—Foreign speakers.
  | English language—Rhetoric—Study and teaching—Foreign speakers. |
  English language—Composition and exercises—Study and teaching—Foreign speakers. | Teachers, Foreign—United States. | English teachers—United States.
Classification: LCC PE1128.A2 I35 2019 (print) | LCC PE1128.A2 (ebook) | DDC 808/.0420869120973—dc23
LC record available at https://lccn.loc.gov/2019025845
LC ebook record available at https://lccn.loc.gov/2019025846

For Mom and Dad
Letizia

Para minha mãe, Maria Aurora Correia Figueiredo
Sergio

Contents

Foreword..ix
  Kate Vieira

Acknowledgments xiii

Introduction: Framing, Tracing, and Complicating the
  Experiences of US Immigrant Teacher-Scholars.............1
  Sergio C. Figueiredo and Letizia Guglielmo

1 Being First: Motivation or Albatross 17
  Chloe de los Reyes

2 Tenemos que hacer la lucha: Reflections of Latinas in
  Rhetoric and Writing Studies 43
  Lizbett Tinoco and Jennifer Falcón

3 Desi Girl Gets a PhD: Brokering the American
  Education System with Cultural Expectations 57
  Ashanka Kumari

4 Writing to Name: Documents, Movement, and
  Disruptions of a New Filipino Immigrant
  Teacher-Scholar 79
  Peter Mayshle

5 A Right to My Language: Personal and Professional
  Identity as a "First Generation" Teacher-Scholar-
  Rhetorician 102
  Letizia Guglielmo

6 Choosing English: Crafting a Professional Identity as
  a College Professor.....................................122
  Natalia Kovalyova

CONTENTS

7   Literacy, Rhetoric, Language Barriers, and Academia:
    A Journey of Knowledge and Identity 139
    Estefany Palacio

8   From Orality to Electracy: A Mystery 159
    Sergio C. Figueiredo

INDEX 185
EDITORS 191
CONTRIBUTORS 193

Foreword

Kate Vieira

In the nightmare of the late 2010s in the United States, migrant lives, in particular those of migrants of color, are newly threatened. The rapid and haphazard changes to immigration policies since 2017 seem aimed at fomenting large-scale chaos and fear, across DACA (Deferred Action for Childhood Arrivals) recipients, refugees, those with protective status, families seeking asylum, and countless others, including—and it is horrifying to type the words—infants and toddlers. I am in the final stages of revising a book about transnational families separated across borders. In this draft, I find myself insisting, again and again, on the fact that migrants are human beings. Apparently, it bears repeating. What is at stake, what has always been at stake, is our shared humanity.

In this context, *Immigrant Scholars in Rhetoric, Composition, and Communication* offers an intellectual, aesthetic, and political balm. The first- and second-generation transnational scholars who have contributed to this volume teach readers what it can mean to write and teach amidst the roiling social context of global mobility. In doing so, they remind us—and remind us just in time—that writing has the potential to be a humanizing practice.

Literacy, it's important to point out, is not always humanizing, especially where migration is concerned: literacy has been used to racially engineer the US population (Ngai); to homogenize an unruly immigrant workforce (Graff); to restrict and regulate immigrant rights (Vieira); to "co-naturalize" language and race, thereby reinforcing white supremacy (Rosa and Flores); and to otherwise perpetuate immigrants' "legal, economic, and cultural exclusion" (Wan 35), including recent proposals to renew the racist legacy of literacy tests for legal entry (a policy that makes about as much sense as a border wall).

Immigrant Scholars in Rhetoric, Composition, and Communication both acknowledges such abuses and offers other, more empowering ways of doing literacy. It lets readers in, for example, to a moment in school when one is speaking the way one knows how to speak and, in a small heartbeat, one realizes one's speech—the speech that flows through one's body and blood, the speech of one's mom, dad, familiars—suddenly becomes a "problem" to be fixed (Guglielmo, this volume). In this way, this book joins scholarship that reimagines language and literacy education not from a monolingual, but from a translingual and community-based, perspective (e.g., Alvarez and Alvarez). It shows how, for example, in the skilled hands of Latina faculty, composition pedagogy can resist white supremacist interpretations of literacy (Tinoco and Falcón, this volume). That is, this book both lays bare injustice and offers possibilities for change: in one chapter, the author shows how official migration papers tried to define him, but how, *hah!*, he defined the papers instead (Mayshle, this volume).

These and the other chapters in *Immigrant Scholars in Rhetoric, Composition, and Communication* are unique in that they offer more than point-counterpoint in the ongoing ideological struggles over language and literacy in transnational lives. The volume's value also lies in its stories. The complexity and thoughtfulness of these accounts put to shame the simplistic and racist narratives currently circulated in US policy and practice. Consider the story that underlies the policy of separating children from caregivers at the US-Mexico border, which can be summed up in one brute, unimaginative, if-then clause: *If you don't want your children taken, then don't come here.* This story is so poorly composed, so underdeveloped in relation to context and plot and human complexity, so impoverished in its conception of who counts as "you" and who counts as "we" and what kind of world constitutes "here," that if it weren't written in papers—in the visas, green cards, passports, and laws that can grant or deny the right to be treated as a human being in the United States—most of us would probably be happy to ignore it. But we can't. Because this story, whose meanings are now indelibly branded into the tender developing consciousnesses of children, is backed up by an army of one of the most powerful nations in the world.

Immigrant Scholars in Rhetoric, Composition, and Communication tells better, more fully human, more intellectually rigorous stories. It meets force with words. In these pages, readers are asked to imagine or to remember the following: being asked about one's English on official forms (Kovalyova); being slotted or not into ESL classes and unraveling the associated stereotypes (de los Reyes); moving among orality, literacy, and electracy (Palacio); embodying the legacy of one's parents' rural homeland (Figueiredo); experiencing both gender oppression and gender empowerment across continents, generations, and social classes (Kumari). These writers couple the art of first-person storytelling with a theoretically grounded communal vision of a more just world, participating in composition and rhetoric's robust legacy of justice-oriented literacy narratives, from Villanueva to Young to Richardson to Gilyard and others.

In writing their stories as transnational scholars—risky subject positions—these authors invite readers into discursive worlds marked by both the volatility of borders and the instability of language itself. Such work takes equal parts vulnerability, bravery, and mad skills. It takes both theory and art. In this way, the writers in this volume are contesting the use of literacy as brute force. And they are shining a bright, clear light by which to navigate a path forward.

This is an important gift. Because writing not only says; in the saying, it also does, a fact that has its liberatory roots in Freire and Lorde. *I wrote this essay,* for example, and *This is my experience in the world* are both statements and actions. They set into motion certain relationships. They break silences. Their words act as a bridge.

Writing, perhaps especially personal writing like the stories readers encounter in this book, can say loudly and in capital letters, *NO*. And it can also hold a reader's hand and lowercase-explain all the ways in which it says *yes*.

Which is a long way of saying the volume before you is an invitation to participate in our shared undertaking of writing and educating for peace in troubled times.

Works Cited

Alvarez, Sara, and Steven Alvarez. "'La biblioteca es importante': A Case Study of an Emergent Bilingual Public Library in the Nuevo U.S. South." *Equity and Excellence in Education*, vol. 49, no. 4, 2016, pp. 403–13.

Freire, Paulo. *Pedagogy of the Oppressed (Revised)*. Continuum, 1996.

Gilyard, Keith. *Voices of the Self: A Study of Language Competence*. Wayne State UP, 1991.

Graff, Harvey. *The Literacy Myth: Cultural Integration and Social Structure in the Nineteenth Century*. New York, Transaction Publishers, 1991.

Lorde, Audre. "The Transformation of Silence into Language and Action." Paper delivered at the Modern Language Association's Lesbian and Literature Panel, Chicago, Illinois, Dec. 1977.

Ngai, Mae. *Impossible Subjects: Illegal Immigrants and the Making of Modern America*. Princeton UP, 2004.

Richardson, Elaine. *PHD to PhD: How Education Saved My Life*. Parlor Press, 2013.

Rosa, Jonathan, and Nelson Flores. "Unsettling Race and Language: Toward a Raciolinguistic Perspective." *Language in Society*, vol. 46, no. 5, pp. 621–47.

Vieira, Kate. *American by Paper: How Documents Matter in Immigrant Literacy*. U of Minnesota P, 2016.

Villanueva, Victor, Jr. *Bootstraps: From an American Academic of Color*. National Council of Teachers of English, 1993.

Wan, Amy J. *Producing Good Citizens: Literacy Training in Anxious Times*. U of Pittsburgh P, 2014.

Young, Vershawn Ashanti. *Your Average Nigga: Performing Race, Literacy, and Masculinity*. Wayne State UP, 2007.

Acknowledgments

Projects like these rarely come to successful completion without the contribution of many people, including the NCTE team. We wish to thank Kurt Austin for seeing promise in this work, as well as our two anonymous reviewers for their generous, thoughtful, and generative feedback that allowed us room to develop ideas, prompted us to engage more consciously and critically with other scholars in the field, and undoubtedly helped us to make this work better. We also thank Bonny Graham for her help shepherding this project through the final stages of production.

We thank our students and colleagues of many years with whom we have shared both the personal and the scholarly and because of whom we have grown and continue to grow as teachers and scholars. We specifically want to thank colleagues who showed us continued encouragement and support as we developed this project: Jeanne Bohannon, Miriam Brown Spiers, Jennifer Dail, Lydia Ferguson, Katarina Gephardt, M. Todd Harper, Laura McGrath, Michelle Miles, Mary Lou Odom, Christopher Palmer, Ashley Shelden, Sheila Smith McKoy, and Lara Smith-Sitton.

We would like to thank each of the contributors to this collection for their dedication to the project over many years, their many insights and thoughtful reflections throughout the writing and revision process, and their willingness both to share their personal histories and to add their voices to this important conversation.

And finally, we express thanks to each other for creating space to tell these stories, for imagining the possibilities of this work, for a mutually beneficial collaboration grounded in this shared experience, and for each other's friendship.

Introduction
Framing, Tracing, and Complicating the Experiences of US Immigrant Teacher-Scholars

Sergio C. Figueiredo
Kennesaw State University

Letizia Guglielmo
Kennesaw State University

This collection of stories from US immigrant scholars of rhetoric, composition, and communication began with a conversation in 2015. Over lunch, we shared personal stories about our experiences with institutional language practices that forced us to negotiate our personal and professional identities and liminal spaces while navigating insider-outsider status as students, teachers, scholars, and professionals. In each story we shared, we saw ourselves engaging with what Carmen Kynard, in *Vernacular Insurrections: Race, Black Protest, and the New Century in Composition-Literacies Studies*, describes as "the presence of many different languages in our classrooms, . . . multiple sets of epistemologies and discursive identities" that shape how we speak, write, and develop ways of being in language (18). As we broke bread and shared our personal narratives, we realized that we shared some common approaches to our scholarly work, even as we moved in different directions with our research and teaching. From this conversation, we started brainstorming how we might develop a collection to explore and interrogate how US immigrant scholars—first and second generation—in rhetoric, composition, and communication contribute to the ongoing conversations surrounding language and communication practices currently being debated in professional journals and other edited collections (Kells, Balester, and Villanueva; Young; Good and Warshauer; Robbins, Smith, and Santini; Donehower, Hogg, and Schell; Bawarshi et al.; Guerra; Ruiz and Sánchez; Vieira).

Our goal was and remains focused on addressing the narratives of first- and second-generation US immigrant scholars in these three fields to explore the significance of the personal that transnational scholars bring to their pedagogical and scholarly work. The broad approach we take in editing this collection is partially grounded in cross-cultural studies as they exist (or have existed) in societies around the globe. As such, this collection represents a contemporary application of George Kennedy's methodology of "comparative rhetoric," a method designed with four overarching objectives:

1. To identify what is universal and what is distinctive about US immigrant scholars' approach to teaching and scholarship in rhetoric, composition, and communication;

2. To take another step toward formulating a general theory of rhetorical awareness in language and communication practices among US immigrant scholars, even as it is applied in different forms across cultures;

3. To develop and test structures and terminology that can be used to describe rhetorical practices cross-culturally; and

4. To apply what has been learned from comparative study to contemporary cross-cultural communication. (cf. Kennedy 1)

These objectives are most apparent in the work we have compiled in this collection and in the theoretical lenses through which the contributors have developed their respective chapters. For instance, when we released the call for chapters for this collection in the summer of 2015, we left the theoretical framework of the collection open. This was an intentional choice grounded in an ethic of care,[1] an ontological experience that resists the urge to funnel authors into a single theoretical perspective. To have done so would not have allowed us to encourage the wide range of theoretical approaches developed in the essays or the diverse motivations found in the authors' narratives. This diversity of theoretical framework and method is, we believe, part of

Introduction

what makes this collection a unique contribution to the field, as it allows readers an opportunity to compare how individual US immigrant scholars position themselves within their respective institutions. In this sense, this collection employs the rhetorical strategy Casie Cobos et al. call "interface," in that it moves away from "prescriptivist and singular definitions of 'cultural rhetoric/s' and instead toward a discussion of the multiple and varied ways in which 'culture' and 'rhetoric' come together, overlap, and move apart"; it aims to "displace the notion that cultural rhetorics must be the exclusive realm of minoritized and racialized subjects" and to "contribute to the sustainability of cultural rhetorics conversations in rhetoric, composition, technical communication, and related areas of research and practice"; it is an attempt to articulate and situate how we use our terms of inquiry to clear a path "for emerging cultural rhetorics scholars" to participate "in our commonplace disciplinary practice of interrogating concepts and our uptakes of them so that we not take these terms nor our agendas for them for granted" (141). The essays in the following pages work in the mode of personal narrative but resist the neoliberal temptation to advocate for a passive theory of social justice grounded in self-interest and personal responsibility. Rather, these chapters use the personal as a starting point for advancing collective and institutional change through active theories of social justice,[2] and contribute to the reflexive practices and methodologies of cultural rhetorics work described by Malea Powell et al. in "Our Story Begins Here: Constellating Cultural Rhetorics" and Phil Bratta and Malea Powell in their introduction to a special issue of *Enculturation*, "Entering the Cultural Rhetorics Conversations."

Embodiment, Affect, and the Ethic of Experience

For all of the issues raised in this collection, perhaps one of the more significant revelations is the authors' experiences as lived, embodied, and affective. What we see in these essays are detailed accounts of bodies moving alongside, between, and across social, cultural, political, and institutional environments.[3] What binds these accounts together is a sense of how, in Sara Ahmed's terms, "the accumulation of affective value shapes the surfaces of bodies and worlds" (121). While the concept of "borders" has long been a part of rhetorical scholarship, with a recent revival in scholarly responses to sociocultural and sociopolitical public policy debates, the narrative approach presented in this collection is an ecological (vis-à-vis a situational) one that demonstrates how the authors' experiences bleed and circulate across social fields.[4] For readers who aim to find some form of understanding about US immigrant scholars' experiences as students, teachers, scholars, and professionals, we hesitate to support common epistemological readings of these essays. Yes, these chapters speak of how the authors have come to know and intentionally position themselves within various institutions (academies, nationalities, etc.); questions of how we know what we know, what is persuasive, and the legitimate status of certain kinds of knowledge abound in this collection. Still, as editors, we want to emphasize that readers should also supplement these kinds of epistemological readings with ontological ones. In our view, to overlook that these are incomplete narratives would lead to misreadings and errors in judgment. These narratives address the encounters of various US immigrant scholars who explicate the personal, ontological experiences and relations that continue to move and circulate across social fields. These chapters are not only statements of subjectivist experiences; they are also glimpses into ontological experiences enmeshed in the spatial mobility of migration. As a whole, this collection speaks less to a mastery of identity and more to the process of negotiating the encounters and relations through which the authors have attuned themselves to the dynamic unfolding of experience.[5] The meaning and significance of such a reading names a category of ontological being (-in-the-world).[6]

An ontological reading of this collection would be one that recognizes these experiences as ordinary affects, with each detailing, in Kathleen Stewart's words, "a surging, a rubbing, a connection of some kind that has an impact" and that is "not about one person's feelings becoming another's but about bodies literally affecting one another and generating intensities: human bodies, discursive bodies, bodies of thought, bodies of water" (128). The pedagogical implications of such a reading are many, including a recognition that both human and nonhuman actors play a role in the affordances generated by personal, collective, institutional, and material (i.e., papers; cf. Vieira) encounters. With each encounter, the authors acknowledge relations to their respective environments and the ongoing process of attuning themselves to those environments in productive and inventive ways, and by doing so, we hope this collection contributes to the kind of work that Cobos and colleagues ask to make "apparent how cultural rhetorics is embodied and employed theoretically and methodologically," both within and beyond scholarly contexts (150).

The roles that embodiment and affect play in the ways the authors approach their narratives are ethical ones, working between and across the intimate and the impersonal (e.g., institutional), the personal and the collective (e.g., communities—national, disciplinary, etc.).[7] Ethic here is used not only to refer to a particular construction of identity or character, but also to the modes of being that each author addresses by examining their intimate and impersonal encounters and relations; these modes of being reflect a state of mind and body (in the broadest possible sense)[8] that guides their methods and practices across contexts. It is an ethic that may be explicit, but is more often implicit in addressing how we inhabit the uncertainty of each experience in a way that "can never be exhausted by linguistic expression ... partly because no two people in the same situation will have had exactly the same experience of it" (Massumi 11–13). As readers move through these chapters, we encourage them to consider how the authors play with the linguistic constraints of each essay and maneuver across those constraints to use language in a manner that offers a sense of how each author navigates the excesses of their various experiences as US immigrant scholars.[9]

Tracing Narrative Pathways

In the sections that follow, we introduce each of the narratives shared by this collection's contributors to illustrate the range of experiences that lead US immigrants, US-born children of immigrants, and immigrant children to professional work in rhetoric, composition, and communication and to theorize those experiences in what we see as a multivocal response to and engagement with both public and academic conversations. Collectively, these narratives function as counterstory, disrupting those public and academic conversations in varied and complex ways that resist stereotypes about language and literacy, unsettle mandates for fixed identities, and extend our definitions of first generation in the academy. Yet individually, even within this collection, each chapter, each author resists a single story (see Kumari). In this sense, the stories collected in this volume respond to Aja Martinez's plea for a proliferation of counterstories—counter to "majoritarian or stock stories"—that "serve the purpose of exposing stereotypes, expressing arguments against injustice, and offering additional truths through narrating authors' lived experiences" (51). As editors of this collection and authors of this introduction, we recognize that our presentation of the chapters in the specific order before you may privilege one reading of those experiences, offering, perhaps, a particular narrative framing at the outset and a gesture toward application and praxis at its conclusion. However, we invite readers to consider how the narratives both engage with one another and resist hasty conclusions both as individual chapters and as a collective. Moreover, we want to emphasize that these narratives present only a sample of the range of experiences that US immigrants bring to their work and that they do not represent a panacea. As Letizia Guglielmo theorizes elsewhere, we welcome re-collection of the chapters and continued disruption of dominant narratives that engage with the ecologies of this intellectual exchange.

In "Being First: Motivation or Albatross," Chloe de los Reyes examines the circumstances that led her to a career in composition studies, highlighting the role that labels such as "first," "special," and "deficient" have played and continue to play in her life as a child, then as a student, and now as a teacher of writing. Like other contributors to this collection, pursuing a graduate degree in composition studies becomes for de los Reyes a process of exploring identity and place. This chapter narrates her understanding of how multiple ways of being, speaking, and writing clearly influence her teaching and allow her to ask questions that prompt readers to confront the lasting influence and power of early labels. Visually, de los Reyes performs counterstory throughout the narrative by alternating scholars' voices or versions of dominant narratives with her own voice to amplify, disrupt, and demonstrate multiplicity and multivocality.

Aiming to complicate Bourdieu's idea of cultural capital in "*Tenemos Que Hacer La Lucha:* Reflections of Latinas in Rhetoric and Writing Studies," Lizbett Tinoco and Jennifer Falcón discuss competing language ideologies and their early and alternating inculcation in family and school environments as the foundation for their work as young Latina scholars in rhetoric and composition studies. Analyzing how their experiences as first-generation undergraduates at universities in different regions of the country with very different academic cultures also shaped their language experiences, Tinoco and Falcón describe consciously coming to terms with the varied ways in which standard language ideologies (SLI) have shaped their classroom language practices and how they, as Latina instructors, can resist and change some of these practices.

Focusing the lens on the experience of first-generation doctoral students in rhetoric and composition studies through her dissertation project, Ashanka Kumari, in her chapter "Desi Girl Gets a PhD: Brokering the American Education System with Cultural Expectations," explains that although the journeys to our careers contain rich complexities, the paths those of us who identify as working-class, children of immigrants, and/or first-generation college students have taken are often misinterpreted or narrowly understood. Kumari argues that despite the personally rewarding parts of attaining a US education, cultural expectations and competing literacies create tension and feelings of imposter syndrome in both academic and familial settings, calling on teacher-scholars in rhetoric and composition to interrogate our own privileging of certain literacies.

A mixed-media piece organized around various official documents gathered for his permanent residency application in the United States, Peter Mayshle's chapter, "Writing to Name: Documents, Movement, and Disruptions of a New Filipino Immigrant Teacher-Scholar," illustrates how papers give tangibility to the tensions between naming and identity, positionality and fluid subjectivity, native and non-native discourses, and questions of location, border crossing, and in-between-ness. Drawing from Pierre Bourdieu's claim that the "imposition of a name . . . is to signify to someone what he is and how he should conduct himself as a consequence" (120, emphasis in original), Mayshle asks, what does it mean, for the composition and rhetoric scholar, to signify, to name oneself? What does it mean for one's students? As Mayshle illustrates, naming can never be "clear-cut" or "unequivocal."

Extending this discussion of naming, Letizia Guglielmo, in "A Right to My Language: Personal and Professional Identity as a 'First Generation' Teacher-Scholar-Rhetorician," narrates moments in her education and professional work in rhetoric and writing studies that serve as touchstones for shaping language, literacy, and identity. Articulating and engaging with what Carmen Kynard describes as "intellectual rootedness in [our] own histories" (13), Guglielmo describes her Italian heritage and cultural identity as both advantage and limitation in the eyes of those defining and naming her language and identity, her insider and outsider status as a citizen and a scholar.

In Chapter 6, "Choosing English: Crafting a Professional Identity of a College Professor," Natalia Kovalyova presents an autobiographical study of the intricate intertwining of professional identities of non-native English-speaking faculty and a campus language policy, noting the latter's assumptions about language proficiency and a rhetorically constructed equation between primacy and effectiveness in fulfilling professional duties. Kovalyova offers counterstory as a method for revealing the "deeply entrenched stereotypes and biases" that policies like these represent.

In "Literacy, Rhetoric, Language Barriers, and Academia: A Journey of Knowledge and Identity," Estefany Palacio addresses her experience of acculturating to a new national culture and way of life while simultaneously adapting to an increasingly networked (technologically) world. Framed by multiple definitions of migration as metaphor, Palacio's chapter marks a transition in the immigrant experience as it parallels expanding modes of discourse and reflects on the ongoing process of pursuing a career trajectory as a teacher-scholar in rhetoric and writing studies.

In the collection's final chapter, "From Orality to Electracy: A Mystory," Sergio Figueiredo presents a snapshot of how his personal experience has come to inform his professional work within "an extended network of meanings" (Ulmer 87) across (inter)national, multilingual, and transmediated communicative modes. Much like the Azorean immigrants Vieira describes in *American by Paper*, Figueiredo's parents were of the first generation in their families to learn to read and write, and this literacy was what facilitated their immigration to the United States in the 1970s. Figueiredo's reflective piece argues, as a fitting bookend to the collection, that few, if any, immigrant scholars are "embodiments" of a singular, collective experience, even if patterns exist across individual experiences.

Complicating Future Trajectories

In recognizing that we both had individual stories bound up with histories as children of immigrants that led us to pursue rhetoric, composition, and communication studies as fields of study and as professional work, we imagine how "little" narratives like ours and those of our contributors might be useful to counter and complicate "master" narratives regarding literacy, language policy, and identity within the field.[10] Bringing together these narratives, this collection offers an expanded story about what it may look like to be a scholar in rhetoric, composition, and communication studies, what it may mean to be a first-generation academic, and perhaps, more significantly, how the liminal spaces that we often occupy may lead us to both reify dominant systems of language and literacy and to be disciplined by them. In the paragraphs that follow, we articulate moments of reflection in our individual stories that raise questions for readers and prompt intervention in our scholarship and pedagogy.

In her study of literacy narratives, Kara Poe Alexander explores the dominance of the "literacy success story" both in scholarship and in classroom practice (623). Engaging with the narratives collected here, we prompt readers to consider how the narratives of first- and second-generation immigrant scholars help to resist or to complicate dominant success narratives in productive ways. How can these narratives disrupt our teaching and scholarly work? How can they contribute to current conversations in our fields? Scholarship, Alexander explains, already moves to complicate the success narrative, yet assignments often gloss over this complexity and unwittingly reiterate the success narrative (624). How might sharing these narratives with students help to expand their understanding of "success" and inform the ways we talk about literacy, language policy, and citizenship within and beyond our classrooms? What does it mean for instructors to assign and to evaluate literacy narratives when their own stories of literacy may not follow a dominant archetype of success? How can counternarratives, like the ones collected here, become risky both for us and for our students while also creating generative space for intellectual exchange?

These narratives also make salient the gatekeeping and disciplining nature of institutional language practices that require continued performance of Americanness and citizenship. For many contributors, these performances began in early education with required ESL courses, often arbitrarily assigned, yet contributors also indicate that this policing and legitimizing is continuous for bodies marked as other, reinforcing an inherent racism and/or xenophobia in these institutional practices. Perhaps more significant are the questions these narratives raise regarding precisely who sanctions our language and literacy practices as legitimate, as these "tests" are often implemented outside of official policy and by peers and strangers alike. How might we engage students in productive conversations about how dominant ideologies about literacy and language policy often mask our everyday practices of "legitimizing" citizenship and community ethos? As teacher-scholars, many of this collection's contributors participate in this process of gatekeeping in some way by teaching in these fields while also attempting to disrupt policy and conversations concerning literacy and language. Their narratives call us to consider when the authors' own literacy, legitimacy, and citizenship have been questioned, when (if ever) they are sanctioned to participate in the gatekeeping that is institutional literacy.

As teacher-scholars, what we may glean from this collection regarding US education as an institution and the role of school in negotiating identity certainly can inform both our classroom practices and the risks we may ask our students to take in those spaces, particularly when those risks involve issues of language, literacy, and citizenship. Contributors articulate important con-

Introduction

nections between attaining "American" education and influencing family status and the challenges of navigating embedded literacies of the US education system. Contributors reveal that this process of "figuring out," of finding US identity, often happens in a school setting. School, in turn, both for young students and for academic professionals, exists as a space of negotiation, prompting readers to consider how we can better envision our classrooms as places where that kind of negotiation happens, and how that negotiation is significantly connected to our theorizing of rhetoric, composition, and communication. Part of this negotiation, this collection's authors reveal, includes the process of naming—naming ourselves, naming our race, ethnicity, and citizenship, naming our language and literacy practices, and being named in myriad ways by those around us and by institutions we inhabit. How do these varied and repeated acts of naming offer us an opportunity to consider their intersection with systems of power in our classrooms and in our professional work?

Beyond theorizing school as a space, contributors engage with issues of place, migration, and movement throughout their individual stories in ways that contribute to and extend conversations regarding rhetorical theory and practice. Authors recognize a fluidity in their language practices, their literacies, and the identities that inform their work in rhetoric, composition, and communication. This recognition is identified, in some cases, as the result of journeys of migration, immigration, and assimilation, yet it is similarly the result of early exposure to multilingual exchange and varied contexts. These experiences become particularly significant within a US context, as they often run counter to our institutional practices and political realities regarding literacy, language, and citizenship as fixed, constant, finished. Bi- or multilingualism can be read as a problem rather than an asset within this space, one that may result in language loss and/or relinquishing one language by claiming another. Paired with fluidity, shifting, and movement, then, are boundaries, borders, displacement, and liminal spaces that raise questions about "home," community ethos, and the extent to which language and identity are bound up in community identity. In narrating moments when they deliberately formed identity to appear—to become—more (US) American, more marketable, more legitimate, contributors reveal the extent to which dis-identification with families, communities, and identities (Alvarez 31–32) may be a necessary part of that process.

As Juan Guerra reminds us, in complicating our analyses and interpretations of transnational students, teachers, and scholars,

> we need simultaneously to acknowledge and to extend the work of the various scholars ... in ways that tactically and strategically serve our theoretical, research and educational needs. The payoff ... will not only provide us with greater insight into the challenges our students encounter in translingual, transcultural, and transnational contexts; it will also inform the theoretical perspectives and the methodological tools we develop and use, as well as the research sites we select, when we work to better understand the varied ways in which language and cultural differences intersect in a transnationally volatile world. (132)

It is our hope that this collection will help move this process forward and spur research into the connections between the personal and the collective in ways that further complicate attempts to universalize each of our respective experiences and to situate cultural rhetorics research as the exclusive domain of any single group.

Notes

1. "Ethics of care" is a theory of well-being dealing with individual and collective ontological experience and with questions of how to respond to others in social relationships. While normative care ethics focus on "maintaining" relationships, non-normative care ethics acknowledges that disrupting the habits that maintain certain relationships may also contribute to the long-term social well-being of a given community, particularly in response to social injustices. See Nel Noddings's *Caring: A Feminine Approach to Ethics and Moral Education* and Carol Gilligan's *In a Different Voice* for a more extensive primer on the ethics of care.

2. For an extended discussion of the distinctions between passive and active theories of social justice, see Jared Colton and Steven Holmes, "A Social Justice Theory of Active Equality for Technical Communication."

3. See Carol Hanisch's "The Personal Is Political: The Women's Liberation Movement Classic with a New Explanatory Introduction."

4. For an extended discussion of the concepts of "rhetorical ecologies" and "circulation," see Jenny Edbauer's "Unframing Models of Public Distribution: From Rhetorical Situation to Rhetorical Ecologies" and Laurie E. Gries and Collin Gifford Brooke's edited collection, *Circulation, Writing, and Rhetoric*. See also Chris Mays's "From 'Flows' to 'Excess': On Stability, Stubbornness, and Blockage in Rhetorical Ecologies."

5. For more on ambience and the *kairos* of "unfolding," see Thomas Rickert's *Ambient Rhetoric*.

6. See Rickert's "Circulation-Signification-Ontology" in Gries and Brooke's *Circulation, Writing, and Rhetoric*.

7. For more on the connections between the intimate and impersonal, see Lauren Berlant's *Cruel Optimism*; Melissa Gregg and Gregory J. Seigworth's *The Affect Theory Reader*; Nigel Thrift's *Non-Representational Theory: Space, Politics, Affect*; Kathleen Stewart's *Ordinary Affects*; Brian Massumi's *Parables for the Virtual: Movement, Affect, Sensation*; and Eve Kosofsky Sedgwick and Adam Frank's *Shame and Its Sisters: A Silvan Tomkins Reader*.

8. See Brian Massumi's foreword to his translation of Gilles Deleuze and Félix Guattari's *A Thousand Plateaus: Capitalism and Schizophrenia* (xvi).

9. Some of this phrasing is derived from Massumi's work in *Politics of Affect* (12–13).

10. Cf. Jean-Francois Lyotard, *The Postmodern Condition: A Report on Knowledge*; Victor Vitanza, "Three Countertheses: Or, a Critical In(ter)vention into Composition Theories and Pedagogies"; Beth Daniell, "Narratives of Literacy: Connecting Composition to Culture."

Works Cited

Ahmed, Sara. "Affective Economies." *Social Text*, vol. 22, no. 2, 2004, pp. 117–39.

Alexander, Kara Poe. "Successes, Victims, and Prodigies: 'Master' and 'Little' Cultural Narratives in the Literacy Narrative Genre." *College Composition and Communication*, vol. 62, no. 4, 2011, pp. 608–33.

Alvarez, Steven. "Brokering the Immigrant Bargain: Second-Generation Immigrant Youth Negotiating Transnational Orientations to Literacy." *Composition Studies*, vol. 3, no. 3, 2015, pp. 25–47.

Bawarshi, Anis, Juan C. Guerra, Bruce Horner, and Min-Zhan Lu, editors. Special Issue on "Translingual Work in Composition." *College English*, vol. 78, no. 3, 2016.

Berlant, Lauren. *Cruel Optimism*. Duke UP, 2011.

Bourdieu, Pierre. *Language and Symbolic Power*. Edited by John B. Thompson, translated by Gino Raymond and Matthew Adamson, Harvard UP, 1991.

Bratta, Phil, and Malea Powell. "Introduction to the Special Issue: Entering the Cultural Rhetorics Conversations." *Enculturation: A Journal of Rhetoric, Writing, and Culture*, no. 21, 2016, http://enculturation.net/entering-the-cultural-rhetorics-conversations. Accessed 1 Feb. 2019.

Cobos, Casie, Gabriela Raquel Ríos, Donnie Johnson Sackey, Jennifer Sano-Franchini, and Angela M. Haas. "Interfacing Cultural Rhetorics: A History and a Call." *Rhetoric Review*, vol. 37, no. 2, 2018, pp. 139–54.

Colton, Jared, and Steven Holmes. "A Social Justice Theory of Active Equality for Technical Communication." *Journal of Technical Writing and Communication*, vol. 48, no. 1, 2018, pp. 4–30.

Daniell, Beth. "Narratives of Literacy: Connecting Composition to Culture." *College Composition and Communication*, vol. 50, no. 3, 1999, pp. 393–410.

Donehower, Kim, Charlotte Hogg, and Eileen E. Schell. *Reclaiming the Rural: Essays on Literacy, Rhetoric, and Pedagogy*, Southern Illinois UP, 2012.

Edbauer, Jenny. "Unframing Models of Public Distribution: From Rhetorical Situation to Rhetorical Ecologies." *Rhetoric Society Quarterly*, vol. 35, no. 4, 2005, pp. 5–24.

Gilligan, Carol. *In a Different Voice: Psychological Theory and Women's Development*. Harvard UP, 1982.

Good, Tina LaVonne, and Leanne B. Warshauer, editors. *In Our Own Voice: Graduate Students Teach Writing*. Pearson, 2007.

Gregg, Melissa, Gregory J. Seigworth, and Sara Ahmed, editors. *The Affect Theory Reader*. Duke UP, 2010.

Gries, Laurie E., and Collin Gifford Brooke, editors. *Circulation, Writing, and Rhetoric*. Utah State UP, 2018.

Guerra, Juan C. *Language, Culture, Identity, and Citizenship in College Classrooms and Communities*. Routledge, 2016.

Guglielmo, Letizia. "Introduction: Re-Collection as Feminist Rhetorical Practice." *Remembering Differently: Recollecting Women's Rhetorical Narratives*, edited by Lynée Lewis Gaillet and Helen Gaillet, U of South Carolina P, in press.

Hanisch, Carol. "The Personal Is Political: The Women's Liberation Movement Classic with a New Explanatory Introduction." *Women of the World, Unite! Writings by Carol Hanisch*, Jan. 2006, www.carolhanisch.org/CHwritings/PIP.html.

Kells, Michelle Hall, Valerie M. Balester, and Victor Villanueva. *Latino/a Discourses: On Language, Identity, & Literacy Education*. Boynton/Cook, 2004.

Kennedy, George Alexander. *Comparative Rhetoric: An Historical and Cross-Cultural Introduction*. Oxford UP, 1998.

Kynard, Carmen. *Vernacular Insurrections: Race, Black Protest, and the New Century in Composition-Literacies Studies*. State U of New York P, 2013.

Lyotard, Jean-François. *The Postmodern Condition: A Report on Knowledge*. U of Minnesota P, 1979.

Mays, Chris. "From 'Flows' to 'Excess': On Stability, Stubbornness, and Blockage in Rhetorical Ecologies." *Enculturation: A Journal of Rhetoric, Writing, and Culture*, vol. 19, 2015, http://enculturation.net/from-flows-to-excess.

Martinez, Aja Y. "A Plea for Critical Race Theory Counterstory: Stock Story versus Counterstory Dialogues Concerning Alejandra's 'Fit' in the Academy." *Composition Studies*, vol. 42, no. 2, 2014, pp. 33–55.

Massumi, Brian. Foreword. *A Thousand Plateaus: Capitalism and Schizophrenia*, by Giles Deleuze and Félix Guattari, translated by Brian Massumi, U of Minnesota P, 1987, pp. xvi.

———. *Parables for the Virtual: Movement, Affect, Sensation*. Duke UP, 2002.

———. *Politics of Affect*. Polity, 2015.

Noddings, Nel. *Caring: A Feminine Approach to Ethics and Moral Education*. U of California P, 2003.

Powell, Malea, Daisy Levy, Andrea Riley-Mukavetz, Marilee Brooks-Gillies, Maria Novotny, and Jennifer Fisch-Ferguson. "Our Story Begins Here: Constellating Cultural Rhetorics." *Enculturation: A Journal of Rhetoric, Writing, and Culture*, no. 17, 2014, http://enculturation.net/our-story-begins-here. Accessed 1 Feb. 2019.

Rickert, Thomas. *Ambient Rhetoric: The Attunements of Rhetorical Being*. U of Pittsburgh P, 2013.

———. "Circulation-Signification-Ontology." *Circulation, Writing, and Rhetoric*, edited by Laurie E. Gries and Collin Gifford Brooke, Utah State UP, 2018, pp. 300–307.

Robbins, Sarah R., Sabine H. Smith, Federica Santini, editors. *Bridging Cultures: International Women Faculty Transforming the US Academy*. UP of America, 2011.

Ruiz, Iris D., and Raúl Sánchez. *Decolonizing Rhetoric and Composition Studies: New Latinx Keywords for Theory and Pedagogy*. Palgrave Macmillan, 2016.

Sedgwick, Eve Kosofsky, and Adam Frank, editors. *Shame and Its Sisters: A Silvan Tomkins Reader*. Duke UP, 1995.

Stewart, Kathleen. *Ordinary Affects*. Duke UP, 2007.

Thrift, Nigel. *Non-Representational Theory: Space, Politics, Affect*. Routledge, 2008.

Ulmer, Gregory L. *Internet Invention: From Literacy to Electracy*. Longman, 2003.

Vieira, Kate. *American by Paper: How Documents Matter in Immigrant Literacy*. U of Minnesota P, 2016.

Vitanza, Victor J. "Three Countertheses: Or, a Critical In(ter)vention into Composition Theories and Pedagogies." *Contending with Words: Composition and Rhetoric in a Postmodern Age*, edited by Patricia Harkin and John Schilb, Modern Language Association, 1991.

Young, Morris. *Minor Re/Visions: Asian American Literacy Narratives as a Rhetoric of Citizenship*. Southern Illinois UP, 2004.

CHAPTER ONE

Being First: Motivation or Albatross

CHLOE DE LOS REYES
Crafton Hills College

> When I work with words, as in this essay, I'm alternately revealing some truths about myself and exposing some truths about others—some happy, some not-so-happy, some vital, some less so. Truths in these parts isn't stable, isn't fixed for all time.
> —JOE AMATO

> First (adj): coming before all others in time, order, or importance.
> Special (adj): different from what is normal or usual; especially: unusual in a good way : better or more important than others.
> Deficient: (adj): not having enough of something that is important or necessary.
> —Merriam-Webster's Dictionary

In American English, being "first" most often signals winning, privilege, or best. For first-generation academics, however, this term has two tongues. At home it says pride, while outside of the home, it says newcomer, outsider, and likely deficient. And even in these two spaces, the tongue splits, for, at home, pride is coupled with pressure—pride in being the first to achieve the very American value of receiving education in English at an American university, but also pressure to succeed, as this now-assigned role raises the status of the entire family. Likewise, outside the home, the newcomer often is celebrated, marked as special (though in a strangely colonial way), but the undertone of deficiency is clear, as the insiders offer to show her the right path (theirs), how to fit in with them, and how to master their language, thus creating a different kind of anxiety about shedding those outsider markers as quickly as possible and in that process pummeling her identity. In these settings, I am at once celebrated as a "first" or "special" one who has made good even as I recognize that these labels mark an understory of deficiency.

It is this language of *first, special,* and their oftentimes companion *deficient* that this chapter interrogates as it highlights the role these labels have played and continue to play in my life—as child, then as student, and now as teacher of writing. However, telling this story of labels is difficult because as soon as I begin, listeners start to nod, to appear to already know my story even better than I do, so much so that they jump in to correct it, to align it with a master narrative. This is both surprising and frustrating, for it seems to elide all that I have come to understand about context, fluidity, identity, and language.

And so, much like Aja Martinez in "A Plea for Critical Race Theory Counterstory: Stock Story versus Counterstory Dialogues Concerning Alejandro's 'Fit' in the Academy," I too am "compelled to describe these experiences coupled with knowledge provided by other scholars who have found it necessary to speak from marginalized spaces like mine" (34) because more often than not, I—and others like me—are spoken for and spoken about by those who are deemed "experts" by the academy, "experts" who often inhabit wildly different realities and experiences from those they are studying. I would like to challenge the master narratives by telling my own story, and I choose the method of (counter) storytelling because "[s]tories, parables, chronicles, and narratives are powerful means for destroying mindset" (Delgado 2413). I'd like to offer my voice as an authority on my own life and experiences, and it is my hope that this chapter and my story bring more nuanced meaning to the many labels often attributed to me.

Coming to America

I was born in Iloilo, a city on the island of Panay, which is part of the group of islands called Visayas that rests in the center of the

Being First: Motivation or Albatross

Philippines. My first language is Ilonggo, although I eventually learned to speak Tagalog, as most Filipinos do. In fact, growing up, I was surrounded by many languages, or variations of them. Sometimes the distinction was in the way people said things—in the accents, as when my mom spoke in Karay-a whenever she was in her hometown in Cabugao; other times, not only would the accent shift but so would the words themselves, so I knew to say *kahig* instead of *tiil* for feet when visiting my grandma's cousins in San Miguel but to say *siki* when visiting her other cousins in Dumarao. Other times, accents, letters, and words seemed to change altogether, so I barely understood what was being said, as when Lola Nany, my grandfather's sister, would come visit and she and my grandpa would speak in Aklanon (or Akeanon), and in their variation, the letter *L* somehow morphs into vowels. When watching television, however, we switched again because most of the programming was in either English or Tagalog. So, as a child, I constantly moved in and out of many registers and languages, long before I began to learn about multi- and translingual theories. It was just one of the ways children acquired and adapted to the languages those around them used.

With this background, I moved to the United States three months shy of my thirteenth birthday, and immediately the blurred and contradictory meanings and uses of *first, special,* and *deficient* began to unfold. In the Philippines, moving to America[1] branded us as special in that our family joined all of those who addressed the gap between the middle and upper class by moving to the United States, where class assignments were not so rigid and where they could earn more money and offer their children better lives. So moving to the United States was special—in fact, many Filipinos are convinced that anything American is far superior—but it also meant that the Philippines was somehow deficient and that we immigrants were in turn deficient for having Filipino origins.

Special or not, I didn't want to move. I was perfectly happy with my life. I didn't think there was anything wrong with where and how I lived. We were middle class by Filipino standards, so I went about my life relatively "unchallenged, unquestioning," much like Peter Mayshle (this volume). We owned our own home; we owned a car (which was not too common); my parents had college degrees and held office jobs. My sisters and I had the opportunity to attend a private Catholic school and to take ballet and piano lessons, and our parents were even able to hire maids and nannies. Occasionally, we got to enjoy certain things that not many others could—to fly away on vacations and have "American" things like apples and chocolate.

However, my parents decided we'd move, mainly because they wanted all of their children to earn college degrees. College tuition had become very expensive in the Philippines. Despite what we had, my parents thought it wouldn't be enough to put three children through universities that would award us degrees good enough to compete with other college graduates, especially in finding jobs. In the Philippines, the best education is reserved for the wealthiest, so moving to another country to work and educate their children is just a thing many Filipino families like ours did during that time. They went to the United States, Canada, and Australia to become nurses and caretakers or to the United Arab Emirates, Saudi Arabia, and Turkey to become domestic help. For a while, women went to Japan to become *japayukis,* or "entertainers." They made these moves for their own lives but even more to create opportunities for their children. Thus, the Philippines has become a country of emigrants and overseas workers, with a big chunk of its GDP coming from overseas foreign workers (OFWs) or *balikbayans*.[2]

I realize now that we also moved because my mother was part of the "Filipino professional nurse labor force" that supplied nurses all over the world (Choy 1). In fact, my mother worked as a nurse in New Jersey before she and my dad were married, and once again in Saudi Arabia after we were born. As with many Filipinos, a degree in nursing was my mom's ticket out of a life with scant possibilities, at least growing up. Unlike my dad, who had lived a fairly middle-class life, my mom had spent her childhood working in the rice fields, so choosing nursing increased her opportunities and allowed her to move up the social ladder. I remember hearing her say once after coming back from a visit in the Philippines how different her life would have been had she not gone into nursing but stayed in the Philippines. "I would've had lots of children that I couldn't afford to feed or send to school," she said.

Being First: Motivation or Albatross

We moved in two groups: *Nanay* (Mom) and my older sister, Apryl, left first, arriving in California in 1993. *Tatay* (Dad), my younger sister, Trish, and I came a year later. *Nanay* and Apryl lived with *Lola*[3] (grandmother) Rose for a year until they got the paperwork set up for us to come. *Nanay* needed to take an exam before she could work as a nurse, so while she was preparing for that, she worked at Price Club serving free samples. It's funny that so many people think living in America must be so special—that it would move us up the social ladder—when my mom, who was a clinical instructor in the Philippines, was serving samples at a warehouse store in the United States. Eventually, my mom passed the nursing boards, and *Lola* Rose managed to get her a job at the convalescent hospital where she worked. *Nanay* worked night shift while *Lola* Rose worked day shift, and because my mom didn't have a car and didn't drive anyway, they traveled together in *Lola* Rose's maroon van, and *Nanay* would sleep in the van while she waited for my grandma to finish her shift.[4] This setup continued for a while. It wasn't ideal but *Nanay* made it work. She made lots of things work.

When *Tatay*, Trish, and I first arrived in the United States a year later, I remember Trish feeling excited (she wanted to go to Disneyland), while I, on the other hand, felt incredible sadness. I missed my grandparents, *Tita* Ambet, *Yayay* Melda,[5] our neighbors, our extended family.[6] In fact, during my first couple of years here, I convinced myself (and tried to convince my parents) that I would go back to the Philippines and go to school there instead. I didn't like that my mom had to sleep in my grandma's van because she couldn't drive, and I was embarrassed having to go to work with my dad, who was inspecting houses. He wasn't particularly good at it, but he hated his first job working at ARCO, so he thought he'd try termite inspection instead. One time, a woman whose house my dad was inspecting felt sorry for me because I sat in the back of the tiny sedan, jammed next to the ladder in the dead heat of the summer, so she gave me a bagful of peaches. I didn't want her peaches, and I especially did not want her pity. My fourteen-year-old self couldn't come to terms with all of the changes my whole family was experiencing. I was both embarrassed and angry when I heard my dad's disappointment about having to start over and being treated like shit; he would always say, "I have a college degree! I used to work in an office. I knew important people."

So the following years were spent adjusting to our new life in the States. I was disappointed a lot. The America I moved to wasn't the America I had imagined it to be. First, it didn't snow like it did in the movies (we lived in Southern California). I remember watching *Home Alone* as a child in the Philippines and imagining Christmases as always cold and snowy. My mom also worked too much. At some point, she worked at three different facilities, and because she didn't drive, we spent a lot of time driving her back and forth between her three jobs. My dad was unhappy with whatever job he had because he struggled with the move and his identity. Much of who he is and was was grounded in the Philippines and on being Filipino.

Our lives changed, but they did not necessarily become easier or better. The five of us lived in a two-bedroom apartment down the street from *Lola* Rose. The plan was for my parents to sleep in the smaller bedroom and the three of us children would share the master bedroom, but somehow my dad ended up on a sleeping bag in the living room or on the couch. Life was rough for a while. My parents fought a lot. My dad wanted to go home and dreams of retiring in the Philippines to this day. I wanted to go home. My mom, however, always convinced us otherwise. She talked about the realities of "home," about the cost of education, about the fact that families often are split up when one or both parents go to work abroad where they can make more money for their families.

Settling In

Another disappointment came when I learned early on that people in America like to put a name or label on everything, something that Kovalyova (this volume) similarly experienced. When Trish and I started going to school, we were put into groups right away by the institution and also by our peers. All of the labels ascribed to us had the same function: they made sure we knew we were special, different, and usually, by inference, deficient. Sometimes the labels made sense, but sometimes they didn't. For instance, for one reason or another, my younger sister was placed in English as a Second Language (ESL) classes, but I wasn't. Trish and I still talk about that time. Neither of us could figure out how the school managed to puzzle out which of us needed to take the ESL test when both of us arrived and enrolled around the same time. We figured it had to depend on whoever was processing our paperwork at the time. Trish talks about how, as a child, being taken out of regular classes to go to her ESL classes was embarrassing. It singled her out as special, but not in a good way. On top of that, she felt that the ESL classes didn't really help her in the long run. Trish already knew how to speak English because the Philippines is a mostly bilingual country,[7] something most of our teachers didn't seem to know or bother to learn. She—we—needed support in other things, such as making friends and understanding the new educational system. Many seemed to think that fixing our English—our grammar, our accents—would solve our issues of fitting in. These external markers, however, are just one aspect of acculturation. In "Literacy, Discourse, and Linguistics: Introduction," James Paul Gee describes how

> Discourses are not mastered by overt instruction (even less so than languages, and hardly anyone ever fluently acquired a second language sitting in a classroom), but by enculturation ("apprenticeship") into social practices through scaffolded and supported interaction with people who have already mastered the Discourse. (7)

Much of what we learned about how things worked we got from our friends, our observations, and our day-to-day interactions.

We eventually figured out how things worked over time and through friends and relatives who were always kind enough to help us out. I've always wondered whether the outcome would have been different if we both had been labeled ESL—and also how that little wrinkle in the system led me to where I am now. Had I been marked as ESL earlier on, pursuing a degree in English might have been out of the question—it would have cemented my feelings of not being good enough. Regardless, both of us have ESL baggage, none of it positive, though I am coming to see it as an asset to me now as a writing teacher because it gives me a personal way to understand my students, in addition to the scholarship that I read.

> In short, the academic ability groups that administrators and school officials describe in purely academic terms manifest themselves among the student population as a set of behavioral and social norms, creating a system of social stratification and categories that are also defined by class, perceived intelligence, behavior, race, and culture. For adolescent second language writers, these institutional categories create predetermined, often rigid school identities based on their membership in an academic track and also in an ELL program. (Ortmeier-Hooper 12)

Even at the age of thirteen, I was acutely aware that my accented English marked me as somehow not good enough. In middle school, I learned the term *FOB* (fresh off the boat) early on. *Fresh off the boat* is a term my classmates and others used for newly arrived (Asian) immigrants who are not yet assimilated into the mainstream culture (Poolokasingham et al. 200). It meant not being good enough, which is ironic considering that *fresh* often means "new" and "good," as in a fresh idea or approach to a problem. But when I was in middle school, *fresh* did mean new but certainly not good. Other students—natives and immigrants alike—were cruel to FOBs. They made fun of us and felt that they were better than we were. And their marker was how we spoke—our accents—and how we dressed. Even more surprising, the earlier arrived Filipinos and Filipinos who were born in the United States were the worst. I thought that perhaps they would take us in and show us how things are done in America. After all, we were *kababayans*—fellow Filipinos—countrymen and -women. But somehow they maintained a healthy distance from those of us who had recently moved. Some were even the first to point out our accents or comment on our "non-American" clothes.

So, much of my middle school years was spent figuring out the American Discourse:[8] how to dress, how to act, how to talk so that I could sit with the "regular" students. Even though I was too young to realize that English was an entryway to the dominant Discourse[9] here in America, I began to realize that sounding less foreign increased the likelihood that people would be nice to me and try to help me. Even without understanding the scholarship of difference, I caught on that I should listen and observe carefully, that the key to not being treated as new, special, and deficient hinged on losing my accent, wearing the right clothes, knowing how to behave—knowledge that still shapes me as I obsess about making "foreigner" grammatical errors when I teach.

Over the years, my accent faded and I sounded more Southern Californian than Filipino, but I still spent a lot of time balancing two identities: an American identity to fit in outside the home and a Filipino identity to appease my parents' fear of raising children who have forgotten their roots. However, my concerns have shifted from losing external markers to balancing internal ones. I put far more thought into what others deem simple decisions because of how they might appear to either my non-Filipino friends or my very Filipino parents and relatives. For example, deciding who to date or whether to live with my parents, both before and after marriage, became hugely complicated as I thought about whose reaction matters most and what I really want to do. When I base my decisions on my Filipino values, I often have a hard time explaining my choices to my American friends, and vice versa. I noticed that my answers shifted depending not only on my audience but also on how I was positioning or identifying myself: Filipino or American.

So the questions of where we should go to college and what we should major in were complicated. Much like Amy Tan, I could see and hear that "[w]hile my English was never judged as poor, compared to Math, English could not be considered my strong suit" (7) because English is my second language. I thought I had a pretty good command of English before arriving in the United States, but over the years, I would hear subtle comments from friends, teachers, school counselors, even colleagues about my accent or about being ESL. Probably most difficult, particularly as I think about it now, is that the comments had nothing to do with being able to understand me—our communication was spot on—and everything to do with marking me as different because of where I placed the accent in a multisyllable word or how I shortened a vowel. And although I'm not terrible at math, I resisted being good at it in an attempt to break the stereotype. In middle school, I became a favorite of Mrs. Miller, my history teacher. She often complimented me on my art and was particularly impressed with my watercolors. Years later, I ran into her at a local grocery store and was severely disappointed when she asked me if I was still good at math.

> I argue that these sorts of archetypes or representations of ESOL learner identity inevitably exist in all institutional settings (and in classrooms) in which students are educated. Prevalent institutional representations promote certain views of learner identity, making these views seem self-evident and unchanging—just the way ESOL students are—while limiting recognition of other views of students or of heterogeneity among them. (Harklau 40)

When I was deciding about college, my parents discussed with me the option of going to a community college first—because it was cheaper—before I transferred to a university. But we also didn't close the door completely. My mom and I attended a financial aid workshop offered by my high school, and I remember sitting there feeling out of place. It felt as though my mom and I didn't belong in that workshop. When the presenter was talking about eligibility assets, my mom asked the presenter about deferred comps, but instead of stressing the "ferred" of *deferred* (deFERRED), she stressed the "de" (DEferred). The presenter couldn't seem to understand what she was talking about, and a kind woman had to step in to "translate" for her. I was mortified. It was little things like this that made me feel that our English marked us as Other, and not a good Other. As Victor Villanueva writes: "Language is also race in America. Spanish is color" (xii). Filipino is also color. At times, our way of speaking dictated how people responded to us, and I suspect this wasn't an isolated experience. Our accented English made us subject to judgment.

Being First: Motivation or Albatross

And I think, many times the way immigrants—people look at immigrants with such a sense of diminishment: as if this person is less than I am, because they've left their country. Well, I actually think they're more than we are, because they're braver. They've gone some other place. They have to operate in another language. How easy would that be? ("Naomi Shihab Nye")

I figured that my mom and dad sacrificed so much for us that the least I could do was actually go to college. I felt a lot of pressure to make this happen. Apryl went back to the Philippines to get her degree—in nursing. She was going to school at the local community college because my parents and she thought that college life here was too hard to navigate. Universities in the Philippines are far more regimented and structured and give students little choice about which classes to take, unlike here in America, where students have a plethora of choices. Culture clash. My parents were also earning dollars[10] now, so they could afford to pay for Apryl's tuition. I thought that she was lucky, getting to go back home, but in retrospect, I don't think I would have liked being away from my mom and dad and Trish. Besides, I didn't want to be a nurse, and that seemed to be the only option if I went home too. Actually, like many Filipino parents, they wanted my sisters and me all to be nurses. The nearly universal demand for nurses, along with the facts that nurses can get working visas easily and nursing is many Filipinos' passport to the United States, leads many Filipino parents to think that nursing, or at least something in the medical field, is one of the few career options their children have. Apryl decided on nursing early on but returned to the Philippines for her training because we couldn't figure out the way into the American school system. We had very few resources or people to ask about how to get into college.

But I didn't want to be a nurse, and neither did Trish. There was quite a bit of pushback from our parents, of course, but I was stubborn. I didn't want to be like all the other Filipinos I knew, at least as far as choosing a career went. Surely, I thought, we can do more than work at a hospital. Trish was less stubborn, so she did go to nursing school, but she eventually settled in a related medical field. I wanted to earn a degree in the food industry or related field and dreamed about opening my own restaurant. I couldn't understand why my parents thought the medical field was our only option. In fact, I often wondered why no one else seemed to question the slotting of certain ethnicities into certain professions.

> I have been thinking about all this lately, about my mother's English, about achievement tests. Because lately I've been asked, as a writer, why there are not more Asian Americans represented in American literature. Why are there few Asian Americans enrolled in creative writing programs? Why do so many Chinese students go into engineering? Well, these are broad sociological questions I can't begin to answer. But I have noticed in surveys—in fact, just last week—that Asian students, as a whole, always do significantly better on math achievement tests than in English. And this makes me think there are other Asian American students whose English spoken in the home might also be described as "broken" or "limited." And perhaps they also have teachers who are steering them away from writing and into math and science, which is what happened to me. (Tan 7)

Undergraduate Years

My application to and eventual acceptance to a local university was unplanned. Trish and I knew we wanted to go to college, but we weren't sure exactly how to do that. And I don't think we did anything extra to prepare ourselves for college, unlike our classmates. We just did things because others did them. We didn't really prepare for SATs or apply to multiple schools. I chose a local university because that's where everyone else seemed to be going. And it was cheaper than most universities. Or so we heard. In fact, in a study done by Kanno and Grosik, "several students revealed that they had been in many ways 'clueless' about essential aspects of the college application process" and that lack of information is a major hindrance to access and successful transition to universities for immigrant ESL students (136).

When I got to college, I was an average student. I was placed in college English and remedial math, but as I took more classes, I realized that I loved English even more than my dream to open a small restaurant. My English classes showed me a different way of looking at things. Looking back now, they helped me to understand America and the rest of the western world. I read *House Made of Dawn* by N. Scott Momaday and Willa Cather's *My Ántonia*. I read Henry James, Edith Wharton, T. S. Eliot, and many others. These stories helped me move beyond what I read in history books. They showed me the complexities of this country, including the plight of immigrants and the different regional cultures. Very seldom did the stories remind me of life back home, and even though there weren't too many books about or written by people like me, I enjoyed them all the same. Come to think of it, there weren't many people like me—Filipinos—in my English classes. One day we were asked to read Sandra Cisneros's *The House on Mango Street* in my Women's Literature course, and I couldn't put the book down—the life Cisneros was describing seemed familiar. It reminded me of the time we finally moved into our own home after living in that cramped apartment.

> The House on Mango Street is ours, and we don't have to pay rent to anybody, or share the yard with the people downstairs, or be careful not to make too much noise and there isn't a landlord banging on the ceiling with a broom. But even so, it's not the house we'd thought we'd get. (Cisneros 3)

Although I did well in my classes, I never excelled. I was not a straight-A student. I was always quiet in class, and professors seemed to favor students who talked, so I didn't stand out. I didn't speak in class because I was terribly shy and was also self-conscious (and still am to this day) about the words that came out of my mouth. I also struggled with writing. It just seemed like it took me longer than others to string together words and sentences. In hindsight, it may have taken me longer to write because I worried that my writing was accented too.

Then one day the professor in my Women Writers course announced in front of the class that my paper on Willa Cather's treatment of land in her novels was excellent. That one little act helped me feel like I was doing something right. It also led to my very first conference presentation, titled "The Treatment of Gardens in Willa Cather's Novels." At the time, I didn't understand the significance of presenting at a conference, nor do I even recall how I managed to put together the proposal, but it was definitely a breakthrough, a sign that I might not be as deficient as I thought I was after all.

Over the years, the combination of my education, time spent in the United States, and the distance from the Philippines has transformed me. I have become increasingly "American." My accent has faded away, although it occasionally creeps back in after long weekends, after an extended time speaking Filipino, or especially when I'm tired. Some years ago, my older sister and her then-fiancé decided to have their wedding in the Philippines, so the whole family went back to the Philippines for the first time in ten years, and I was struck by the realization that home didn't feel like home anymore. It felt like we were vacationing in a whole new country. Seemingly simple acts, such as getting in line to buy bread, were a bit confusing. Even more telling, I had a hard time speaking in my native tongue. I worried that I might have gone too far—only to be reminded when I returned to the States that I was not American enough.

> I have never stopped trying to assimilate. And I have succeeded in all the traditional ways. Yet complete assimilation is denied—the Hispanic English professor. One can't get more culturally assimilated and still remain other. People of color carry the colony wherever we go. Internal colonialism: a political economy, an ideology, a psychology. (Villanueva xiv)

> I am walking back and forth between these two roles I play and trying to look for the one that I truly belong to. What is my identity? I am stuck on the intersection of the two paths and

do not know what to do and where to go. I need a direction to follow. These conflicts between my two cultures and natures make me undefined. So I am seeking and trying my best to figure a way out and put these pieces of the puzzles together. (Yang 53)

Graduate School

When I received my bachelor's degree in English literature, I had no idea what to do with it, so I decided to keep going to school. I applied and was accepted into the master's in English composition program at the same university where I received my BA. I went to grad school because I didn't know what I wanted to or could do with my degree—I wasn't sure about teaching, and I felt like I wasn't a good enough writer to work in a writing-heavy field. But deep inside, I think I went to grad school because I wanted to improve my writing: to know grammar, to know perfect English. At the time, I didn't really know what composition studies was. It sounded like it was related to English and writing, so I figured it was going to help me somehow. But there was a part of me that was rebelling against these labels. Much like Amy Tan, I felt annoyed, deficient, and challenged, and pursuing a graduate degree in composition studies became my way of trying to figure out who and what I am and my place in the world.

The first time I encountered ESL scholarship was in my Issues in Tutoring Writing course. It gave a language to the issues I had struggled with for many years. My studies helped me piece together all of the things I was interested in about writing and my personal experiences as an ESL student. The body of ESL scholarship we read in that course gave me the means to talk about and make sense of my experiences. I didn't necessarily like being an ESL student, but at least it showed me that my sisters and I weren't alone. For example, even though I recognize that Richard Rodriguez's work has been critiqued for its effect on affirmative action, at the time I was heartened to read of Rodriguez's discovery of Richard Hoggart's scholarship boy, and along with Rodriguez, I found that "my education finally had given me ways of speaking and caring" about my experiences. "According to Hoggart, the scholarship boy grows nostalgic because he remains the uncertain scholar, bright enough to have moved from his past, yet unable to feel easy, a part of a community of academics" (Rodriguez 74). Joseph Harris describes a similar experience:

> A similar irony, I think, describes my own relations to the university. I was raised in a working-class home in Philadelphia, but it was only when I went away to college that I heard the term working class used or began to think of myself as part of it. Of course by then I no longer was quite part of it, or at least no longer wholly simply part of it, but I also had been at college long enough to realize that my relations to it were similarly ambiguous—that here too was a community whose values and interests I could in part share but to some degree would always feel separate from. (133)

In graduate school, I came across a plethora of labels that described me: English as a Second Language (ESL), nonnative English speaker (NNES), First Generation, Generation 1.5, and, more recently, multilingual. The labels helped me understand who I am. They too branded me as "special," but once again they also marked me as "deficient" as they spoke of ways to make me better, make me become part of the dominant group. Being labeled "different" once again seemed to limit me, and I really worried about whether I had any right to think of a future as a teacher of other writers. In fact, when my Issues in Tutoring Writing professor suggested that I apply to become a tutor at our campus writing center, I quickly responded that I didn't think my grammar was good enough for that. Fortunately, she suggested that grammar was not the only important element in tutoring writing. I did nervously become a tutor, only to discover that I knew more than I thought I did. Also, I can see now that my experiences were critical in shaping my thinking about language acquisition and discourse community membership—but at the time, my difference seemed only to point to deficiency.

In the twenty-first century, the rhetorical construction of second language writers continues to be complicated. Second language writers have historically been identified by labels and categories, including ESL, LEP, EFL, ELL, ESOL, bilingual, nonnative speaker (NNES), L2, and Generation 1.5. The terms move in and out of favor based on a number of factors from political correctness to educational policy. But all of these terms mask the complexity of second language writers' identities. (Cox et al. xv)

I saw theory, practice, and personal experience come together in the writing center. My confidence started growing in this space as I worked with other student writers. I saw that I could ask good questions that helped writers move toward their goals, and I could learn at the same time. I saw that seeing me work with American English gave confidence to other students who looked like me. But I also was never far from the deficient label. One day, for example, as I sat down and introduced myself to a student with whom I would be working, I was taken aback when he responded, "You're Chloe? My tutor? In writing? In English?" So much for my specialness! To make matters even more confusing, he was also Asian! I couldn't figure out what his issue was with me. Did he think Asian students can't be tutors of English? His reaction shouldn't have surprised me, though, for I had expressed that same doubt when I was first invited to become a tutor.

Nonnative English-speaking teachers (NNESTs), in particular, despite their professional training, are often marginalized in the profession by the native speaker fallacy; that is, an idealization of the native speaker as the best teacher of English. (Zheng 31)

Constantly confronted with this image of himself, set forth and imposed in all institutions and in every human contact, how could the colonized help reacting to his portrait? It cannot leave him indifferent and remain a veneer which, like an insult, blows with the wind. He ends up recognizing it as one would a detested nickname which has become a familiar description. The accusation disturbs him and worries him even more because he admires and fears his powerful accuser. "Is he not partially right?" they mutter. "Are we not a little guilty after all? Lazy because we have so many idlers? Timid because we let ourselves be oppressed?" Willfully created and spread by colonizer, this mythical and degrading portrait ends up by being accepted and lived with to a certain extent by the colonized. (Albert Memmi qtd. in Osajima 153)

Teaching Composition

> This story, along with the many other stories that I will tell here, will serve not as micro-instances of campus racism but as macro-pictures of political life in American universities. I intend for these stories to offer a context for the ways in which we must understand and rupture whiteness, racial violence, and the institutional racism of our disciplinary constructs in composition-rhetoric as central to the political work we must do. (Kynard 1)

> The institutional racism in which students and faculty must daily think and act is always very real and moving according to the specificity of two directions: the local situation and the national tenor of the moment. (Kynard 2)

Upon receiving my MA, I have continued to teach—as an adjunct—in several departments at the same institution: in the English department's First-Year Composition Program, in the Educational Opportunity Program (EOP), and occasionally for the International Extension Programs. My research interests and training have always centered on second language or multilingual writers, so I was specifically hired by all three sites to work with students who have backgrounds similar to mine. In some ways, it felt good to be hired by my alma mater, especially by the English department. It made me feel that I was "worthy" of teaching in a composition-heavy program, one that actually puts into practice much of what we discussed during my graduate studies.

However, I continue to question my place as a teacher of composition. It doesn't help that I occupy a rather status-less position as an adjunct. I keep thinking about my ESL identity and how my students and colleagues might perceive me. Will they question my expertise? Will they notice my subtle accent? Sometimes I feel as though my native-speaker counterparts have the upper hand, but, then again, I notice that they are beginning to turn to me to knit together what I know about language acquisition with what they know as native speakers or monolinguals. I also think about the many multilingual scholars who write and contribute so richly to the field of English studies.

Early in my teaching career, I heard rumblings about my credibility as an L2 writing instructor because my master's degree is technically in composition studies. Never mind that I was a class and an internship away from a degree with an additional focus on Teaching English as a Second Language and applied linguistics. (I had decided not to take on the additional requirements because grad school was getting too expensive and I needed to just finish.) These rumblers neglected to factor in that I am a multilingual, that I live the life many of them have only read and theorized about in their studies, and that my lived experiences might give me access and insight to things that coursework cannot. Again, I saw how this fixation on labels severely limits the way we perceive people's abilities, knowledge, or expertise. Degrees and labels are fixed, but research interests and learning experiences are fairly fluid. In fact, my interest lies in the space between composition studies and applied linguistics because positioning myself in this way has allowed me to see beyond the rigid lines and boundaries these labels create, to cross over and see issues between these two perspectives—to learn from the other and to create bridges where there would normally be gaps.

I see myself in many of the students I teach. Many of us are firsts—first to arrive or be born in America, the first to go to college. We are special, but sadly, their literacy narratives are riddled with the stigma of being marked as ESL, ELL, NNES, and this subtle—yet powerful—"we feel deficient." A couple of summers ago, as I taught in a Bridge EOP for the second time, a student asked me if I were being "nice" because they were EOP students. When I asked what she meant by "nice," she shyly implied that many teachers think EOP students are somehow not as good as non-EOP students, and she wondered why I would want to teach her and her classmates. I looked around the room and saw myself among them—again first, special. This time, however, I no longer saw deficiency, because I saw "difference in language not as a barrier to overcome or as a problem to manage, but as a resource for producing meaning in writing, speaking, reading, and listening" (Horner et al. 303). Embracing my multilingual self has allowed me to enter a collaborative learning space with my students—to connect with them, to show them that I understand their struggles and how it feels to not quite get it, to not have the language or the words, or even to feel deficient. I am also able to share with them how to move beyond these feelings of deficiency and to use what I know about how language works to explore alongside them not just grammar and correct usage, but also the ways of thinking and being that come with these shifts.

> The very experience of discovering and negotiating my multiple identities as a writer is what helps me relate to my students' ardent desire to be able to write without a marked "written accent," but at the same time what also makes me concerned. Only when educators, L1 and L2 writers and readers, and all members of each discourse community are fully sensitized to these issues will we be able to benefit from every writer's full participation in the community as competent rhetors of English. (Kim 170)

Choosing composition studies has helped me think about who I am; identifying as a compositionist whose lifelong work revolves around multilingual writing and writers[11] allows me to show how the power of the label carries on for me and others like me. It is both motivation and albatross. Labels are helpful, but we are much more complicated than our labels. I get terribly annoyed when others assign me a label that I don't think applies to me or that I don't identify as—at least not in that moment. I remember being annoyed and insulted when a graduate student asked to interview me because she was studying nonnative-speaking (NNS) teachers. I sent her an email saying that even though English is not my first language I don't consider myself an NNS. It may have seemed, and I know the student did not feel ill will toward me; however, once again, the label implied negative things about my ability and place in the academy. But it also showed me that we need these labels to help define our work; for example, we cannot teach "ESL" or "multilingual" if we cannot label our students as

ESL or multilingual. Yet these labels can so easily become traps. Even though they may feel innocent to those doing the labeling, they almost always feel denigrative to those to whom they are being applied (Rafoth 34).

What strikes me now as I work in the field and as I go to conferences is that there are very few people like me there. And I feel out of place, which suggests that the field isn't as open as we say it is. I feel very different. I feel extra self-conscious. I sometimes feel like an onlooker rather than a participant; I talk less, and I walk away frustrated after I hear a native speaker say what I wanted to say but didn't. As Victor Villanueva writes, "I think of how it would be if the number of academics of color actually reflected the demographics of the country" (vii). I am curious as to why compositionists seem to take an either/or stance: either they insist that "writing is writing" and that they don't "see anything wrong" with L2 writers (even though they often send them to writing centers to work on grammar), or they delegate L2 work to linguists. Only a few work together to bring their experiences and research to shape their scholarship or teaching. The transnational work of Horner and colleagues has begun that conversation, but the interchanges remain more frequently a contested rather than a collaborative territory of linguistics and writing programs (see Canagarajah).

It seems to me that composition studies has a long way to go to narrow the gap between theory and practice. Our field often stresses the importance of diversity and equity for our students, we advocate for open access, and we interrogate the powers of language, yet the people in and the actions of our community do not necessarily reflect the ideas we preach. Carmen Kynard says it best:

> It is much safer for us to unfurl the specialized, disciplinary methodologies and vocabularies in which we have been trained rather than turn our analytical gaze onto our institutions and its actors that have maintained calculatingly repressive environments, policies, and climates for students and faculty of color. It is a kind of intellectual activist-work that is quite distinct from the organizational work that we do at bourgeois professional conferences and the scholarship that we most often pursue. (2)

We need to do more than just talk because these "[g]eneral discussions about moral and philosophical principles of equity, equality, or diversity are *no longer good enough*" (Kynard 4, emphasis mine). It has become increasingly hard to be part of a field that doesn't quite practice what it preaches. It is also hard to convince students that they can make it if they don't see anyone like them modeling success. As an adjunct working in a two-tiered academic system in the field of composition, I also have experienced this theory and practice divide. On the top tier reside the tenured and tenure-track faculty, the specialists, the WPAs, the policymakers, and the "boss compositionists," whereas on the bottom tier reside the adjuncts, the generalists, and those of us who "only" teach first-year composition courses. Labels are powerful, and they often dictate to which tier you belong and how you can contribute, and it is demoralizing.

I hope that this chapter can encourage our field to rethink its understandings of the power of labels. When students hear "good, but," they hear the "but" more powerfully than they hear the "good." We need to continue to work on this, to talk about this, to be open to diverse people—not just pay lip service, but consciously work on the language and labels we use. And we need to do this for teachers as well as students. If we act on what we know about identity and language, we will be careful about what we are asking both faculty and students to do in composition, how much we welcome or exclude or require our students to change for the convenience of those in power. If the guidance counselor who appeared not to understand my mother at the financial aid workshop had been interested in the translingual view of language that Mullin, Haviland, and Zenger describe, had he been curious about her question rather than dismissive of her accent, he might have helped both of us feel college-worthy rather than deficient. Most important, I hope we can move beyond just theorizing about inequities in our institutions and effect change so that we do not fall into the trap of embracing "our scholarship on race [and language] but do not speak or write against the ways our institutions actively reproduce inequality" (Kynard 3).

Notes

1. Filipino's often refer to the United States simply as "America," the place they are moving to or have moved to, a practice I'm replicating here.

2. According to Thomas-Brown and Campos in "A Qualitative Analysis of the Lived Experiences of a Small Group of Filipino Immigrants," Filipinos working overseas can be broadly categorized into either overseas foreign workers (OFWs) or *balikbayans*. OFWs are those on temporary work contracts, whereas *balikbayans* are those who have immigrated to other countries to live permanently.

3. *Lola* Rose was my dad's aunt, but most Filipinos refer to our elders—related or not—as *Lolo* (Grandpa) or *Lola* (Grandma) and *Tito* (Uncle) or *Tita* (Auntie).

4. Interestingly, even though she was very successful as a nurse and boasted about getting perfect scores on all versions of the written driving test, my mom never made it to the actual driving test and still does not drive. Many Filipino women I know don't drive in the States. I suppose it's because women typically don't drive back in the Philippines, or at least they didn't when I was growing up.

5. *Tita* is equivalent to "Auntie"; *Yayay* is our family's term of endearment for our nanny.

6. Many Filipinos live with extended family. My mom's sister and aunt both lived with us in the Philippines.

7. According to the Philippine government website, English is one of its official languages, while Filipino is its national *and* official language ("About the Philippines").

8. Here, I am using James Paul Gee's term from "Literacy, Discourse, and Linguistics: Introduction." Discourse, according to Gee, is "a sort of 'identity kit' which comes complete with the appropriate costume and instructions on how to act, talk, and often write, so as to take on a particular role that others would recognize" (7).

9. Dominant Discourses, according to Gee, are Discourses of which a mastery will provide social advantage (8).

10. Because of the generally high US dollar to Philippine peso exchange rates and other economic factors, earning dollars usually means stronger spending power.

11. I am not entirely comfortable "identifying as a compositionist" or claiming specialization in multilingual writing and writers, for I am frequently reminded that, with only an MA, I am a marginal colleague both on campus and when I present at national and international conferences.

Works Cited

"About the Philippines." *Republic of the Philippines: National Government Portal,* https://www.gov.ph/about-the-philippines. Accessed 23 Mar. 2018.

Amato, Joe. "Family Values: Literacy, Technology, and Uncle Sam." *Passions, Pedagogies, and 21st Century Technologies,* edited by Gail E. Hawisher and Cynthia L. Selfe, Utah State UP, 1999, pp. 369–86.

Arva V., and P. Medgyes. "Native and Non-Native Teachers in the Classroom." *System,* vol. 28, no. 3, 2000, pp. 355–72.

Canagarajah, Suresh. *Facebook Transnational Writing* (Group). Accessed 27 Sept. 2015.

Choy, Catherine Ceniza. *Empire of Care,* Duke UP, 2003.

Cisneros, Sandra. *The House on Mango Street.* Vintage Books, 1984.

Cox, Michelle et al. Introduction. *Reinventing Identities in Second Language Writing,* edited by Michelle Cox, Jay Jordan, Christina Ortmeier-Hooper, and Gwen Gray Schwartz, National Council of Teachers of English, 2010, pp. xv–xxvii.

Delgado, Richard. "Storytelling for Oppositionists and Others: A Plea for Narrative." *Michigan Law Review,* vol. 87, no. 8, 1989, pp. 2411–41.

Gee, James Paul. "Literacy, Discourse, and Linguistics: Introduction." *Journal of Education,* vol. 171, no. 1, 1989, pp. 5–17.

Harklau, Linda. "From the 'Good Kids' to the 'Worst': Representations of English Language Learners across Educational Settings." *TESOL Quarterly,* vol. 34, no. 1, 2000, pp. 35–67.

Harris, Joseph. *A Teaching Subject: Composition since 1966.* Utah State UP, 2012.

Horner, Bruce, Min-Zhan Lu, Jacqueline Jones Royster, and John Trimbur. "Opinion: Language Difference in Writing: Toward a

Translingual Approach." *College English,* vol. 73, no. 3, 2011, pp. 303-21.

Kanno, Yasuko, and Sarah Arva Grosik. "Immigrant English Learner's Transition to University: Student Challenges and Institutional Policies." *Linguistic Minority Students Go to College: Preparation, Access, and Persistence,* edited by Yasuko Kanno and Linda Harklau, Routledge, 2012, pp. 130-47.

Kim, Soo Hyon. "Burning Each End of the Candle: Negotiating Dual Identities in Second Language Writing." *Reinventing Identities in Second Language Writing,* edited by Michelle Cox, Jay Jordan, Christina Ortmeier-Hooper, and Gwen Gray Schwartz, National Council of Teachers of English, 2010, pp. 169-73.

Kynard, Carmen. "Teaching While Black: Witnessing and Countering Disciplinary Whiteness, Racial Violence, and University Race-Management." *Literacy in Composition Studies,* vol. 3, no. 1, 2015, pp. 1-20.

Martinez, Aja Y. "A Plea for Critical Race Theory Counterstory: Stock Story versus Counterstory Dialogues Concerning Alejandra's 'Fit' in the Academy." *Composition Studies,* vol. 42, no. 2, 2014, pp. 33-55.

Matsuda, Paul K. "The Myth of Linguistic Homogeneity in U.S. College Composition." *College English,* vol. 68, no. 6, 2006, pp. 637-51.

Mullin, Joan, Carol Peterson Haviland, and Amy Zenger. "Import/Export Work? Using Cross-Cultural Theories to Rethink Englishes, Identities, and Genres in Writing Centers." *Reworking English in Rhetoric and Composition: Global Interrogations, Local Interventions,* edited by Bruce Horner and Karen Kopelson, Southern Illinois UP, 2014, pp. 150-65.

"Naomi Shihab Nye: Your Life Is a Poem." *On Being,* 28 July 2016, https://onbeing.org/programs/naomi-shihab-nye-your-life-is-a-poem//.

Ortmeier-Hooper, Christina. "The Shifting Nature of Identity: Social Identity, L2 Writers, and High School." *Reinventing Identities in Second Language Writing,* edited by Michelle Cox, Jay Jordan, Christina Ortmeier-Hooper, and Gwen Gray Schwartz, National Council of Teachers of English, 2010, pp. 5-28.

Osajima, Keith. "Internalized Oppression and the Culture of Silence: Rethinking the Stereotype of the Quiet Asian-American Student." *Race, Class and Gender in the United States: An Integrated Study.*

Edited by Paula S. Rothenberg, 7th ed., Worth Publishers, 2007, pp. 152–55.

Poolokasingham, Gauthamie, et al. "'Fresh off the boat?' Racial Microaggressions That Target South Asian Canadian Students." *Journal of Diversity in Higher Education,* vol. 7, no. 3, 2014, pp. 194–210.

Rafoth, Ben. *Multilingual Writers and Writing Centers.* UP of Colorado, 2015.

Rodriguez, Richard. *Hunger of Memory: The Education of Richard Rodriguez.* Dial Press, 1982.

Spack, Ruth. "The Rhetorical Construction of Multilingual Students." The Forum. *TESOL Quarterly,* vol. 31, no. 4, 1997, pp. 765–74.

Tan, Amy. "Mother Tongue." *The Threepenny Review,* no. 43, 1990, pp. 7–8.

Thomas-Brown, Karen, and Annalie L. Campos. "A Qualitative Analysis of the Lived Experiences of a Small Group of Filipino Immigrants." *Qualitative Sociology Review,* vol. 12, no. 1, 2016, pp. 114–41.

Villanueva, Victor, Jr. *Bootstraps: From an American Academic of Color.* National Council of Teachers of English, 1993.

Yang, Jun. "Lost in the Puzzles." *Reinventing Identities in Second Language Writing,* edited by Michelle Cox, Jay Jordan, Christina Ortmeier-Hooper, and Gwen Gray Schwartz, National Council of Teachers of English, 2010, pp. 51–53.

Zheng, Xuan. "Translingual Identity as Pedagogy: International Teaching Assistants of English in College Composition Classrooms." *The Modern Language Journal,* vol. 101, no. S1, 2017, pp. 29–44.

CHAPTER TWO

Tenemos que hacer la lucha: Reflections of Latinas in Rhetoric and Writing Studies

LIZBETT TINOCO
Texas A&M University–San Antonio

JENNIFER FALCÓN
University of California, San Diego

The number of Latinx students entering higher education has significantly increased in the last few years. According to a Pew Hispanic Center' study published in 2013 by Richard Fry and Paul Taylor, the number of Hispanic[1] students ages eighteen to twenty-four enrolled in college has more than tripled since 1993. However, the study claims that Hispanics are not earning as many four-year degrees compared to other groups, mostly because more Hispanic students attend two-year colleges and enroll in college part-time. At the University of Texas at El Paso (UTEP),[2] the nationally changing demographics reported in the Pew study do not make much of a difference because the institution already has a large Latinx student body population. UTEP has an estimated 23,000 students, and according to "UTEP Quick Facts," about 78 percent of the student body identifies as Hispanic, and around 5 percent comprises international students from Mexico ("UTEP 2014–2015 Facts"). What differentiates UTEP from other Hispanic-serving institutions (HSIs) in the United States is its unique location and the students' linguistic complexities.

UTEP is located on the US-Mexico border, and students cross the border on a daily basis from Ciudad Juárez, Chihuahua, Mexico, to attend UTEP. Most of the students attending UTEP are from the El Paso or Juárez region, with a small number from out of state or other countries. Because only a highway and a border fence separate UTEP from Juárez, Spanish is heard everywhere on campus. The linguistic complexities of students at UTEP are rich, and one must step foot on campus or be in a classroom to fully understand these complexities. In addition to having a diverse student population, UTEP celebrates this diversity by promoting professional development workshops aimed at helping instructors to be better prepared to serve UTEP students. UTEP enacts university-wide initiatives aimed at fostering and developing the different knowledge and skills students bring to the classroom through learning communities, community engagement, first-year experience, and student leadership. Plenty of Latinx students at UTEP speak Spanish, but there are many who do not speak Spanish at all. Many students consider themselves fully bilingual in Spanish and English. However, there are also plenty of students who speak Spanglish. On any given day, students at UTEP are code switching and/or code meshing. Due to the linguistic diversity and capital UTEP students bring with them into the classroom, it is important for the field of rhetoric and writing studies to continue research on multilingual students, especially Latinx students, to resist traditional ideas about multilingual students being underprepared for the writing classroom.

Since the conception of UTEP's rhetoric and composition doctoral program in 2004, the faculty have developed a curriculum that focuses on critically analyzing language and culture. Through graduate coursework that takes into account our unique context along the border and our professors' interests, some of our regular courses focus on global rhetorics, cultural rhetorics, and critical race theory. More recently, our program started offering a graduate certificate in Bilingual Professional Writing and started piloting bilingual (Spanish-English) first-year writing courses. Since UTEP is predominantly a Latinx campus, our graduate program affords us the opportunity to bridge the gap between theory and practice. As writing instructors, we grapple with teaching students to think critically about their language practices and the active role in creating knowledge these language practices have in and out of academic discourses.

While we recognize that the lived experiences of Latinx scholars all vary, by sharing our personal histories and experiences with language and our pedagogical practices, we hope to shed light on the ways our personal experiences have shaped us as scholars. As multilingual instructors, we invite you to open up spaces in your classrooms for students to incorporate some of their multilingual literacy practices into their work.

Personal Histories and Experiences

Language ideologies inculcated in us by our families, and how these differed from those ideologies we learned at school at a young age, are what drive our positions as young Latina scholars in rhetoric and composition studies. Scholarly works in translingualism and translanguing provide a space for discussion about the ways in which different languages are present in the classroom. In "Whose Culture Has Capital? A Critical Race Theory Discussion of Community Cultural Wealth," Tara J. Yosso uses critical race theory (CRT) to critique Bourdieu's idea of cultural capital by stating that his ideas "expose White, middle class culture as the standard, and therefore all other forms and expressions of 'culture' are judged in comparison to this 'norm'" (76). Yosso argues that CRT shifts the focus from the dominant White, middle-class culture to the cultures of communities of color. As Latina instructors in rhetoric and composition, it is important for the two of us to share our experiences with language and education to show the array of Latinx experiences. It is our hope that it is beneficial for students and instructors to understand that Latinx experiences are not all the same and cannot be theorized so generally.

Jennifer

Spanish was spoken in my house as a child, but it was never directed at me, a second-generation Mexican American. My parents' first-generation experience as products of an era when English Only was enforced with corporal punishment influenced the amount of Spanish and English they spoke in our house. My parents spoke English to my siblings and me, and often used their first language of Spanish only when talking to my grandparents or our bilingual neighbors. My grandfather spoke only Spanish, and many of my earliest memories revolve around conversations with him in which my bilingual grandmother acted as our translator. These experiences of needing a translator, or simply not fully understanding what was said around me, happened often throughout my childhood. I was born and raised in Los Angeles, a melting pot of cultural and linguistic practices, where hearing not only Spanish but also many other languages everywhere I went was common. It was equally common to witness people struggling to communicate with teachers, cashiers, gas attendants, etc. I grew up comfortable seeing signs and storefronts displaying text that I could not read. My knowledge of the existence of many languages manifests itself in my teaching pedagogies, which specifically encourage my students to see the value in and make use of all of their linguistic capital.

Attending a four-year university was not presented as an option to me when I was a child; there were no discussions about whether I would go to college. There were only expectations. I was told from a young age that after high school I would attend a university and earn my bachelor's degree. My parents attended college but never graduated. They were insistent upon their children graduating because they recognized that career advancement would be difficult without a degree, and I often heard them say that their legacy would be the success of their children. Success was to be measured by education and financial security. This was, of course, not something I understood fully at a young age, but it was as present in my life as the sunshine of Southern California. During my senior year of high school, I applied to many schools, but one visit to Ohio State University in Columbus, Ohio, and I knew where I would be spending my undergraduate years. However, earning acceptance to OSU and learning to adjust and transition to living in the Midwest were two completely different battles. OSU is one of the largest universities in the country. It boasts close to 60,000 students on the main campus. That's about 44,000 undergraduates and roughly 13,000 graduate students. Fliers and recruitment videos highlight the academic programs, the campus lifestyle, and the university's commitment to diversity.

During my time at OSU, the university did what it could to fulfill this promise of building a more diverse experience for students. I was encouraged by the talk of diversity. But arriving in the Midwest from the cultural melting pot that is Los Angeles led to my feeling out of place. For the first time in my life, I truly felt like a minority, and I was hopeful that I would meet people like me when I attended programs sponsored by the office of First Year Experience (FYE). FYE programs and events are designed to help students' transition successfully from high school to college. During my first year, FYE brought authors to campus, held lectures at night that addressed such topics as time management and study skills, and supported various other programs aimed at helping students. A short summer reading list was passed out during orientation, and some of these programs revolved around that list.

One of the books on the summer reading list was Julia Alvarez's *In the Time of the Butterflies*. I eagerly read it and looked forward to Alvarez's visit to the university. I genuinely hoped that discussing her book in class would make me feel at home in a place so different from where I was born and raised. Unfortunately, the book was never discussed at any point in my composition class. I was able to attend a talk and book signing with Julia Alvarez, but no other programs put on that year catered to the Latinx student population. This could be due to the fact that on average, from 2002 to 2014, only 2.5 to 2.9 percent of the overall undergraduate population was Latinx ("Highlights"). Also during this time there was an attempt to recruit a more diverse student body, so numerous student groups received support from the university. The Alpha chapter of Alpha Psi Lambda, the nation's first co-ed Latinx fraternity, often co-hosted events with the university, so the support was there for Latinx students, but in my experience the conversation around diversity focused only on programs that brought minority authors, scholars, and activists to campus. The trouble with some of OSU's diversity initiatives and programming while I was a student stemmed from the fact that they didn't address language. Outside of a Spanish-language class, the issue of bilingualism and multilingualism didn't come up. The programs that FYE hosted focused on helping students succeed at OSU, but these programs never veered outside the goal of pushing students to develop good study habits and make positive lifestyle choices. The percentages of international students and Latinx students suggested that these discussions should take place, and that many of the students enrolled at OSU possessed language practices that aren't often recognized as valuable in Standard Edited American English (SEAE).

Despite the limited focus of FYE programs and the extreme culture shock I experienced moving from Los Angeles to Columbus, I was able to adapt to life in Ohio quickly thanks to those programs. However, what I learned early on was that my peers' expectations of me were based on what they saw in the mainstream media. When they asked to practice their Spanish with me, I couldn't help them. When my classmates were surprised at how well I spoke English or about the quality of my papers, I understood that the common narrative of Latinx students was that we struggle with language. This was embarrassing, because I felt as though I had to fulfill the specific expectations others had of me. I had to explain that I knew how to speak, read, and write only in English.

That dominant image of Latinx students struggling with the English language was troubling to me for numerous reasons. At the time, I didn't understand how my peers who were required to attend FYE events focused on diversity couldn't shake their preconceived notions about the struggles of bilingual students. The idea that bilingual students always struggle with writing and oral communication will hinder us at the university level unless we find ways to demonstrate the value and advantages of bilingual speakers in the composition classroom. I believe that discussing the Alvarez book, which contained short passages and words in Spanish, could have provided an opportunity to explore how language played out in the novel. Did its presence add or take anything away from the narrative? Perhaps then my classmates and I could have discussed language in our own lives and what, if any, advantages there are to being bilingual or multilingual. Simply addressing the issue of language might have clued in some of my peers as to why I might be offended that they assumed I would struggle with writing.

My experiences with the FYE programs and at OSU in general demonstrated the lack of discussion, or inclusion, of language practices outside of SEAE. If FYE and similar programs at other universities could incorporate some of these ideas into their programming, perhaps there could be a shift in the ways in which the next generation of scholars and professionals that graduate from OSU and other universities can be part of the dismantling of these standard language ideologies.

Lizbett

"*No Ingles en la casa*" and, paradoxically, "Spanish only" were phrases I heard plenty of times throughout my childhood. My parents, more specifically my dad, would scold my sisters and me if we spoke English at home. As a result, Spanish became a language we used only at home and to communicate with family. As soon as I got home from school, I had to speak Spanish. To this day, I speak Spanish only with my dad because he never learned how to speak English. At times, my dad regrets not allowing us to speak English at home because he believes that would have helped him learn the language.

As a first-generation Mexican American, I grew up in Oxnard, California, an agricultural town in Southern California. My parents, while picking strawberries, celery, or whichever crop was in season, did not need to know English. Tired of the backbreaking work, my mom decided to start her own housekeeping business, and my older brother and I—only six years old—became her translators. My siblings and I would always translate, whether it was ordering for our parents at fast-food restaurants, reading school notes written in English to our parents, or helping my mom establish her business. What I didn't recognize at the time was how often I engaged in language brokering. In "Brokering Literacies: Child Language Brokering in Mexican Immigrant Families," Steven Alvarez writes, "[T]o language broker is to serve as liaison with influence in exchange between individuals, to partake in an exchange as an active audience assuming creative or independent agency" (5). Alvarez adds, "[L]anguage broker youth consider their translations and interpretations as contributions to the good of the family, as a way of demonstrating care" (3). I recall having a hard time translating from English to Spanish and vice versa, and plenty of times, I didn't know the Spanish version of words in English. These instances of translating are essentially what prompted me to focus on learning both languages since my brother's and my ability to translate for my mom's business had large economic implications for the well-being of our family.

Since Spanish was my home language, English became the language I used only at school. In second grade, I had one of the most traumatic language experiences of my life. My teacher sent a note home recommending that I take speech classes, classes to help remediate my English-language skills. At that age, I probably didn't know how to translate and relate the message to my parents, so they just signed it. As a result, every week I got pulled into a small room with a few other students and we would get drilled on vocabulary. We were constantly reminded that we needed to speak only English at school if we wanted to "properly" learn the language. I quickly became terrified that I would say something wrong, and I was also concerned that I would say something in English with a Spanish accent. This supplemental language course attempted, in essence, to erase any traces of my home language. I feared that Spanish and traces of a Spanish accent that were not acceptable at school would hinder communication with my family at home.

Many Latinx students attend college close to home because there is a sense of responsibility and desire to keep familial bonds strong. As a result, choosing where to attend college was not an easy decision for me. As a young teen, I wanted to be as far away from home as possible. However, I was greatly influenced by my parents. I almost didn't apply to the University of California, Los Angeles (UCLA) because it was too close to home, but my mom would always bring up the fact that when she was growing up in Mexico, UCLA was a name she always heard. I knew how competitive UCLA was, and continues to be, so I applied without ever imagining I would be accepted. When I heard back from all the schools I was admitted to, I had to decide whether to move up to Northern California to attend my dream school, UC Berkeley, or stay close to home and attend UCLA. I decided to stay close to home because of the close relationship I have with my family. Most of my mom's family lives in Oxnard, but my *abuelito, abuelita,* and some *tías* and *tíos* live on the same street as my parents. I didn't want to miss out on family events—birthdays, BBQs, or other celebrations.

I have never once regretted attending UCLA, and I take pride in being a part of the Bruin family. However, my experiences there as a Latina student were a bit rough. From day one, I didn't feel like I belonged. Going from a community and high school with predominantly Latinx students to feeling like an outsider at UCLA was a shock. UCLA, a school that prides itself on being one of the best public research universities in the world, had a student population of approximately 25,000 in 2004, the year I entered, according to their "Common Data Set 2004–2005." Of those students, 3,821 were Hispanic and only 517 were first-time, first-year Hispanic students ("Common Data"). I was fortunate to be one of the 517, but it was rare to see any of the other 516 Hispanic students on campus.

If it weren't for the Academic Advancement Program (AAP), a program for first-generation, underrepresented students, I don't know whether I would have graduated from UCLA. AAP offers peer tutoring in many subjects. I received one-on-one tutoring for my English Composition 3 course, which I later learned most students at UCLA test out of due to high SAT or AP exam scores. English Composition 3 wasn't labeled a remedial writing course, but thinking back and considering what I now know as a scholar, it definitely felt like one. The building where tutoring took place wasn't only for tutoring, but was also a space and location that allowed me to engage with other students of color on campus. Walking into tutoring was always something I looked forward to because it felt like a safe place and much like home on a campus where I felt like a stranger.

I went into UCLA as pre-med, and it wasn't until my second year that I made the switch to English. My experience in the English composition course, along with some comparative literature courses, made me realize the power of language. As a Latina on campus, I never felt as though I was at UCLA due to my academic ability; I always felt like a statistic to boost the university's minority numbers. I can now see how UCLA and its institutional capital instills hegemonic discourses, but interacting with the people I did during tutoring made me realize that I could make a difference to change these discourses by pursuing a degree that would give me access to language practices in higher education. All of my experiences with language and higher education have influenced my teaching pedagogies and research interests as a scholar.

Pedagogical Practices

In *Latino/a Discourses: On Language, Identity, and Literacy Education*, Michelle Hall Kells, Valerie M. Balester, and Victor Villanueva write, "We know. We know of the Latinos and Latinas in our classroom. We know of their linguistic complexity, but we haven't found ways to translate this knowledge into classroom practices that aren't still founded on an assimilationist set of assumptions" (2). When a large number of students in first-year composition (FYC) have different academic preparation and perspectives from those of the traditionally homogeneous "mainstream" student, classroom dynamics shift, calling on instructors at these institutions to take into account the linguistic complexities at HSIs. As a result, we both take on different pedagogical approaches to make sure that our classrooms are linguistically diverse. We understand that standard language ideology has a long history in and outside of the classroom, but we see our positions as new scholars and instructors as an opportunity to continue to do research in this area of rhetoric and writing studies, and to encourage inclusion of diverse language practices in the classroom. Current research tries to embrace diverse linguistic practices, but a gap still exists between the lived experiences of students and their experiences in the classroom. Our goal is to create environments that allow students the freedom to use all of their linguistic capital and rhetorical knowledge, because we view this as beneficial and in no way detrimental to their development as writers.

Jennifer's Practices

The specific practices and activities in my composition classroom vary from class to class. At UTEP some classes are made up of students who are mostly bilingual but who prefer to concentrate on writing and practicing writing in English. Other classes consist of groups of students who fret over grammar and vocabulary because they feel that inconsistencies in those areas impact the effectiveness of communicating their ideas in papers written in English. Students I've taught can typically easily switch between speaking in English and in Spanish. They often use a mix of both in conversation. However, they are usually accustomed to being

Reflections of Latinas in Rhetoric and Writing Studies

limited to writing only in English throughout their writing process. To promote linguistic diversity in my classroom, I attempt to create an environment that places value on the students' diverse linguistic practices.

One way of doing this is to regularly encourage students to work in Spanish if possible during their writing process. Of course, this is a choice the student makes, but I make it clear that they have options. Due to the proximity to Ciudad Juárez, students often take an interest in political and socioeconomic issues that are common in Juárez and the border region, so for students researching and writing about topics relevant to the border area, I encourage them to use sources written in Spanish. This is beneficial not only when students are analyzing sources, but also when students are researching, because they are likely to encounter a different point of view. The use of sources written in Spanish has been especially helpful to students who struggle with beginning to research a topic and/or writing their thoughts and ideas in English. I leave the choice of how to include these sources up to the student. They have the option to directly quote these sources in Spanish or to translate them. In my experience, students benefit from engaging with their topics in the language they feel more comfortable with. This provides the agency to synthesize information on their topic and attempt to use it to strengthen their research. If the assignment calls for students to use credible sources to help them establish ethos and strengthen their analysis or research, then perhaps what matters most is that they are able to connect the information and ideas to the topic, and not that the sources are written in English. If they can successfully synthesize and enter a discourse, they are more likely to write and communicate their thoughts effectively.

This is a brief example of my pedagogical approach, but it is a strategy I see as beneficial to my students. Openly valuing students' diverse linguistic skills helps students become more comfortable in their writing.

Lizbett's Practices

In my classroom, I encourage students to examine their multilingual practices and move away from the monolingual writing they have been accustomed to producing in school. In some of my composition courses, students begin by composing a language narrative, similar to a literacy narrative, that asks them to examine their experiences with language. In this assignment, I invite students to code mesh and incorporate the multiple languages they engage with. I also give students the opportunity to move beyond traditional written narratives by composing a visual or digital narrative instead. I encourage them to think about the various audiences they communicate with inside and outside of the university and how these audiences have an impact on their language practices.

As a response to Alvarez's call to include more ethnography and autoethnography in writing courses, I have students conduct autoethnographic work about their own communicative practices. Students collect data and samples of writing and communication they perform throughout the semester. As Alvarez mentions, projects like these are "rooted in students' real lives," and through this project, my goal is for students to understand that their multilingualism is an asset. Additionally, Alvarez mentions that such "[l]anguage brokering could be emphasized in schools with bilingual students as an untapped potential for empowering students and improving development of crafting voice in writing" (11).

Another crucial aspect of my teaching is to purposefully move away from monolingual texts when assigning readings. I make it a point to include as many multilingual texts and texts by scholars of color as possible. I want my students to see themselves in and relate to the readings we discuss in class. My hope is that by reading the work of such scholars, students get a glimpse of teachers and scholars who advocate for diverse languaging practices in academia, and that students' own communicative practices are valued.

Conclusion

Like many of our Latinx students at UTEP, we both know what it is like to navigate through unfamiliar territory when entering college. According to Beatrice Méndez-Newman's "Teaching Writing at Hispanic-Serving Institutions,"

> Compositionists with little or no experience at Hispanic-Serving Institutions (HSIs) quickly discover that traditional training in rhetoric and composition inadequately addressed the impact of many Hispanic students' sociocultural, socioeconomic, and ethnolinguistic makeup on performance in the writing class and on acculturation into the larger academic community. (17)

Our experiences as students and instructors constantly remind us to incorporate multilingual language practices in our classes. We were fortunate to be in the same graduate program and receive training in research and pedagogy that was always mindful of the diverse community of students at UTEP. Through our practices, our hope is to encourage students in our writing courses to use their languages and lived experiences to effectively communicate with their communities in and out of academia.

Notes

1. We use the term *Hispanic* because it is the term used by this study and the various institutions mentioned in Fry and Taylor's article.

2. Both of us were graduate students at UTEP.

Works Cited

Alvarez, Steven. "Brokering Literacies: Child Language Brokering in Mexican Immigrant Families." *Community Literacy Journal*, vol. 11, no. 2, 2017, pp. 1–15.

"Common Data Set 2004–2005." *UCLA Academic Planning and Budget*. https://www.apb.ucla.edu/Portals/90/Documents/Campus%20Stats/CDS%20Fall%202004.pdf Accessed 20 Apr. 2015.

Fry, Richard, and Paul Taylor. "Hispanic High School Graduates Pass Whites in Rate of College Enrollment: High School Drop-out Rate at Record Low." *Pew Research Hispanic Trends Report*, 2013.

"Highlights of Fifteenth Day Enrollment For the Autumn Quarter 2010." Reporting Student Enrollment. Accessed 20 Apr. 2015.

Kells, Michelle Hall, Valerie M. Balester, and Victor Villanueva, editors. *Latino/a Discourses: On Language, Identity, and Literacy Education.* Boynton/Cook, 2004.

Newman, Beatrice Méndez. "Teaching Writing at Hispanic-Serving Institutions." *Teaching Writing with Latino/a Students: Lessons Learned at Hispanic-Serving Institutions,* State U of New York P, 2007, pp. 17–35.

"UTEP 2014–2015 Facts." *UTEP University Communications.* Web. Accessed 20 Apr. 2015.

Yosso, Tara J. "Whose Culture Has Capital? A Critical Race Theory Discussion of Community Cultural Wealth." *Race, Ethnicity and Education,* vol. 8, no. 1, 2005, pp. 69–91.

CHAPTER THREE

Desi Girl Gets a PhD: Brokering the American Education System with Cultural Expectations

ASHANKA KUMARI

Texas A&M University-Commerce

> *All of these stories make me who I am. But to insist on only these negative stories is to flatten my experience and to overlook the many other stories that formed me. The single story creates stereotypes, and the problem with stereotypes is not that they are untrue, but that they are incomplete. They make one story become the only story.*
>
> —CHIMAMANDA NGOZI ADICHIE,
> "The Danger of a Single Story"

When I was seventeen, I knew I was going to college. I didn't know anything else except that I loved learning and that's what college would offer: more learning opportunities. When my dad was seventeen, he knew he wanted better. For years he had watched as his four older siblings faced financial challenges while acquiring their education post–high school in India. Just as Estefany Palacio's mother assessed their home situation in Colombia (this volume), my dad knew that life in India wasn't going to get better. When a group of friends told him about opportunities to make money working abroad, my dad decided to

---

Portions of this chapter were previously published in her dissertation, *Remaking Identities, Reworking Graduate Study: Stories from First-Generation-to-College PhD Students on Navigating the Doctorate* by Ashanka Kumari, University of Louisville.

take the risk, acquired travel papers to go to Europe, and began the immigration journey to what became his life in America. Instead of attending college, he chose to leave his lower-class family in India and travel to gain financial independence. My dad made it to Greece, where he worked various trades for five years and learned how to speak Greek fluently enough to get his travel papers to take advantage of an opportunity to work at a Greek restaurant in New York City.

After a few years in the United States, my dad acquired a visa to return to India and begin the process of getting married. He and my mother had an arranged marriage; shortly thereafter, my dad left India again, leaving my mother behind for two years while he worked to acquire travel papers for her and a place for them to begin their life together. From what he's told me, he didn't envision a bright life for his future family in India and wanted more than he possessed growing up in India's lower class. My dad earned his US citizenship after this move; my mom, a US citizen today, chose the green card route. I arrived in the world a few years later in Long Island City in Queens, New York, my parents' first child. My dad knew he wanted me to have an education, so he started an education savings fund for me, one that helped me pay for college when the time came.

I think about my dad almost every time I walk into a higher education space. Often, I literally enter or exit these spaces with his voice in my ear as I call to see how he's doing. I describe myself as either at, going to, or going home from school when he asks where I am. In those moments, our topic of conversation is always about my relationship with my education, the one that makes my dad proud of his daughter. I chose to attend college because I didn't think the alternatives were better than continuing my education, which my parents raised me to believe would set me up for the best life. For my dad, foregoing college in India to work in Greece offered a change toward something better.

Our journeys to our careers involve rich complexities, yet the paths of those of us who identify as working-class, children of immigrants, and/or first-generation college students are often misinterpreted or narrowly understood. As Chimamanda Ngozi Adichie argues, single stories of a person or group of people belittle our intricate identities, because one story can't represent all stories and can become an oppressive fiction for an identity group. My dad's immigration narrative is complicated. It reflects perseverance and presents examples of nonlinear literacies that have influenced my upbringing and education so much that I pursued a dissertation project looking at first-generation doctoral students in rhetoric and composition. While my parents understood my getting an education as a path toward upward career and class mobility, I understood it as a responsibility to my parents, a way to create my own financial and job security, a way to carry our family name forward. Pursuing an education became a cultural value beyond my parents' expectations. Here, I reflect on my own life as a child of immigrant parents and a first-generation college student working toward a career as a teacher-scholar in rhetoric and composition. I argue that despite the personally rewarding elements of attaining a US education, cultural challenges create tension and feelings of imposter syndrome in both academic and familial settings.

Growing Up First

I didn't grow up speaking English; Hindi and Punjabi prevailed as the primary languages of my household until I formally learned English when I was around five years old. My dad picked up Greek when he worked in Europe and then found work cooking at a Greek restaurant in Queens, where he didn't need to know English to do his job well. My mom stayed at home with me and my younger brother until I could navigate the dominant language and culture more independently. She perceived her job at the time to be taking care of my brother and me while we grew and prepared for school. When I began elementary school, my mom took free English night classes at a nearby community center and later worked at a baked goods factory. Over the years, our household languages evolved into a hybrid "Hinglish" we still use today.

As my brother and I were growing up, our family watched both American and Indian television, which today influence my pop culture approach to writing pedagogy. In the realm of American television, my mom and I especially loved family sitcoms like *The Cosby Show* and *Full House* that gave us a taste of American values and family life with which we agreed. These shows granted glimpses of what we could expect as I grew up in US society and attended US schools. My mom hoped I would be a good student while always respecting my parents, just like the eldest siblings on these shows. Television programs taught us American cultural literacies. Additionally, TV shows informed my English. My mom's obsession with the popular game show *Wheel of Fortune* taught me my ABCs. On my dad's days off, we played with a See 'n Say toy that coached me through basic vocabulary and sounds while I watched *Sesame Street* or *Barney & Friends*. I also learned how to memorize and write my name, phone number, and address—key pieces of information my parents felt I needed to internalize to survive in school. I learned cultural and academic literacies privileged in the American shows we watched.

However, my multicultural television viewing often created tension between cultural understandings of what literacies I, as an Indian American girl, needed to obtain. Generally speaking, most children raised in the United States grow up watching Disney movies. I, however, grew up watching Bollywood movies. So, while other girls might engage with visions of seeking love in the Western cultural landscape where complicated family relationships and absent parents prevailed, I learned about romance and love through a South Asian lens. Every weekend, the Hindi and Punjabi cinema channels showed newer-released films. These films often preserve and propel ideas of Indian culture and identity through their portrayals of "religious ritual, elaborate weddings, large extended families, respect for parental-authority, adherence to norms of female modesty, injunctions against premarital sex, and intense pride and love for India" (Ganti 43). For my parents, and especially for my mom, having us watch Bollywood movies became one way of protecting and passing on their Indian cultural values. These depictions of cultural values emphasize the ideas that men and paternal figures should be treated and respected as if they are gods, that you should follow your parents' desires for you, and that women belong in the home as the primary caregiver.

Thus, while I learned educational literacies, I also learned household ones. My younger brother, on the other hand, did not live under the same expectations of household literacies. My mom and dad encouraged me to practice and strengthen both my household and my educational literacies under the assumption that later in life, after completing my education, I would follow the traditional path of most Indian girls and have an arranged marriage to a good Indian man, raise my own children, and carry forth our familial traditions and ideals. As I outline later, the acquisition of these literacy practices eventually created tension in my pursuit of graduate degrees. When teacher-scholars in rhetoric and composition consider how students acquire their (multi)literacies, we should also interrogate *why* certain literacies might be privileged over others. Who determines what literacies we get and when?

Sometimes television created unrealistic expectations for my future. For instance, depictions of the large and lavish homes that TV American families lived in felt surreal in comparison to the one-bedroom apartment my family occupied during my childhood in New York City. These portrayals of homes offered another cultural literacy for my parents, who adopted these spaces as their goal for when they saved enough to buy their first house, which occurred while I was attending middle school. Further, TV shows presented single stories about success in the US education system. These representations often lacked images of families who looked like mine. My dad envisions school as highly competitive, perhaps influenced by TV story lines about parents pushing their children to earn high grades and win competitions, but I think he gets this idea from watching too many Scripps National Spelling Bees, which typically feature numerous South Asian children.

"Come here! Come look!" my dad would shout from his recliner in the living room.

"What, Daddy? What's wrong? Oh . . ."

A boy, who is obviously of South Asian descent, judging by his appearance and name, spells *floccinaucinihilipilification* correctly on national television and wins the Scripps National Spelling Bee and all of the amazing scholarships and awards that go along with it.

"Look at that! Why don't you do that?" my dad would interrogate.

"Dad . . . it's not that easy. Those kids memorize the dictionary and are born speaking Latin."

"Why don't you do that?"

"Memorize the dictionary?!"

"If they can do it, so can you."

I tried memorizing the dictionary once. I got to the second page of the letter *A* and quit. Despite his intelligence, my dad underestimates the challenges of the US education system. Like many Asian parents, my dad, since my earliest days of school, has expected me to work hard and compete against children born into higher economic and social privileges, speaking English as their native language, with parents who completed their postsecondary education. Sometimes I worried I would never be good enough until I won a national competition myself; however, my dad's wild dreams for me and my family taught me to engage competitively in my pursuits and do the best work I could possibly do. I consider myself a lucky and fortunate woman to have such an encouraging and supportive father.

Combined, my parents, family friends, television, and educational toys served as some of my early literacy sponsors, or the "agents, local or distant, concrete or abstract, who enable, support, teach, or model, as well as recruit, regulate, suppress, or withhold literacy—and gain advantage by it in some way" (Brandt 166). For me, my parents and their friends operated as agents who both taught me foundational language skills and navigated the complex landscape and forms to get me enrolled in kindergarten. These reflect key literacy practices for immigrant families navigating the US education system. Television programs and educational toys contributed concrete and abstract models that informed my expectations of American cultural and educational norms. Thanks to my dad's faith in my education, by first grade I was reading chapter books and receiving accolades for the amount of reading I did each week. To this day, my dad takes every opportunity to talk about how well my brother and I are doing in school. He brags on us constantly, though he also continues to push us to work harder. "You don't know what real work is yet. You're too soft," he often tells us when we whine about our schoolwork or exhaustion. By example, through his dedication to finding ways to support our family, my dad taught me how to look for knowledge beyond the surface level. He instilled in me an inquisitive nature, to which I attribute my educational successes. "Don't be afraid to ask questions if you don't understand something. Your teachers are there to help you," he told me before I started kindergarten and continues to remind me today when I talk to him on the phone.

My parents, television, and educational toys sponsored the basic literacies that allowed me to begin to navigate the school system that my dad aspired for his children to thrive in. After a few years, I could extend my language skills to help my parents by "language brokering" for them in public spaces outside our home. Steven Alvarez defines language brokering as bilingual speakers "serv[ing] as liaison[s] with influence in exchanges between individuals [with less proficiency], to partake in an exchange as an active audience assuming creative or independent agency" (5):

> For language-minoritized families, the standardized academic English literacy required by schooling necessarily entails language brokering and power inequalities. This ability to redistribute linguistic inequalities permits non-English individuals to broker linguistic capital in the linguistic marketplace, and I argue language brokers profit in a number of ways. Their possession of English in their families signifies Bourdieu's notion of *ethos* as "a sign of status intended to be evaluated and appreciated," a "sign of authority, intended to be believed and obeyed" (66). (Alvarez 10)

In my family, I became the go-to language broker. Because of my early acquisition of the English language, my younger brother by two and a half years picked up a lot of English in his formative years, leaving his Hindi and Punjabi skills weaker by comparison. By second grade, my parents gave me the power to fill out all of our school forms. I would translate, explain each section to my parents, and point them to places to sign. I took power over my education by learning the paperwork game. This control granted me the ability to design my school plan. If I wanted to participate in an extracurricular group or attend a field trip, I simply needed to navigate the form and acquire a signature; as long as it came from school, my parents assumed it would be beneficial for my future. I also took on many parental roles because I wanted to share a similar home experience with my classmates; for instance, I set reasonable bedtimes for my brother and myself and made sure we both got our homework done so that my parents wouldn't have to worry about it when they came home from long days of work; I knew my *dadi ma* (dad's mom) or parents' friends who took care of us wouldn't discipline us this way. As literacy sponsors, my parents gained two educated children; as a language broker, I took back some control over my participation in the system. These practices disrupt the standard notion that the US education system often leaves immigrant and/or first-generation children without control. But power and control take many forms. By amassing language and academic literacies early on, I understood how to move through school on my own terms.

Adapting in Alabama

I realized my difference around age nine. That year, my family moved from New York City to a small town in northern Alabama because my dad found better work opportunities at a convenience store in the South. Devastated and knowing only southern stereotypes, I worried about adapting to what I pictured as a farm life.

"Will I have to take care of pigs?" I asked my mom. "I need you to buy me overalls to fit in."

"I don't think so," my mom would tell me. "We'll be living in an apartment just like we do here. It'll just be a different city. We can't afford a new wardrobe for a while. You should be fine with the clothes you have. Maybe they'll have a different school uniform anyway."

The school I attended in New York required us to wear school uniforms. I never disliked these uniforms because they made getting ready easy in the morning. Honestly, I didn't have much of a personal opinion for or against them when the prompt came up on standardized exam essays; but I digress. I mention these uniforms here because I realize now that what I wore said something about my family, my social position, and my class status. In New York, I never cared what I wore to school. I let my mom buy my clothes and wore whatever she picked out for me. But suddenly, what I looked like began to matter to me. Based solely on my exposure to popular representations of the South through television characters such as Lucy's cousin Ernie from Tennessee on *I Love Lucy* or Stinky Peterson on *Hey Arnold!*, I assumed a certain look would give me cultural capital in my new school and, most important to me, with new friends, to make up for the many I left in New York. I entered my new fourth-grade classroom in Alabama fearing I would immediately be laughed at for my New York accent or lack of overalls. I did feel out of place because of the way I looked, but not because of my clothing—I stood out as the only Brown student amidst a sea of almost all White faces.

That first day, the teacher asked us to brainstorm a list of ideas to preface the next assignment. While I don't remember the specifics of this assignment, I remember that I generated a list rather quickly because of my experiences practicing writing at my former schools.

"Oh, look at this! Ashanka has filled up an entire page already," the teacher exclaimed, holding up my paper to the class.

In that moment, my difference became amplified and I felt my face burning from embarrassment. I worried that I had made a mistake when other students looked at me with "Oh, she's a smarty-pants too" eyes. For the next few years, I focused my energy on blending in and trying to make friends. After careful observation of my classmates, I picked up on what I thought of as key cultural practices in this space and began to enact them. I tried to "speak like a southerner," playing with the new-to-me word *y'all* by casually (and often incorrectly) dropping it into my spoken sentences; drink sweet tea and pretend to enjoy it more than I did; and pledge allegiance to a college football team and dress in their colors on Fridays like my classmates. I attempted to assimilate to my new southern school spaces by creating connections with peers through mimicking what I saw. While I still wouldn't say I've accepted or fully taken on a southerner identity, I developed a strong southern costume that I mentally took on in my performance as a student. Beverly J. Moss draws us to Paul Laurence Dunbar's 1972 poem "We Wear the Mask" to consider the implications of class status on these feelings of "otherness":

> As a way of fitting in, many of us find ourselves "wearing masks" [. . . ,] and trying to erase any racial, ethnic, gender, or class markers that point to our differences. Many of us try to fit into two worlds, wearing a mask in the office, in the

classroom, at conferences, and in publications, and taking it off in the privacy of our homes or when we're with our "friends from home." (161)

During school, I would put on my "I'm a southerner mask" to fit in, and I would take it off at home where I still embodied city ideals. I continually renegotiated and reconsidered my identities as a city child and southern student, as I do today as an Indian American daughter and teacher-scholar. These negotiations became further complicated when the events of September 11, 2001, happened less than a year after our move to the South, intensifying my racial identity in the eyes of fellow students and, for my parents, customers and coworkers, some of whom screamed at them to "go back to your country" and called them "terrorists." No place felt safe or welcoming despite my attempts to fit in.

I finally made a few new friends in middle school. I fit in with the fellow gamers, readers, and, because I elected to learn an instrument, band kids. Unfortunately, my parents, like many South Asian parents, resisted the idea of school dances and sleepovers; they worried that these social events would take time and focus away from my studies, though in actuality they could help me attain social capital among peers. I realized that staying in the school building was the only way I could hang out with my friends, so I joined nearly a dozen extracurricular clubs, which meant I always found a reason to stay at school longer than regular school hours. My parents liked these extra school hours because, along with the scheduling ease they created when negotiating their work schedules with my school schedule, these clubs appeared to represent an extra devotion to my studies in a space they understood as safe. In many ways, these clubs helped me acquire the social, educational, and professional literacies that set me up as a successful college candidate later. I learned a lot about my strengths and weaknesses, pursued a diverse array of interests, and practiced my communication skills. My investment and energy in these organizations afforded me leadership opportunities that eventually led to the kinds of college scholarships I received. Further, I looked forward to school and began to care more about my academic performance; I didn't want to lose access to extracurricular programs because of my grades.

Motivated, I was a model student and eventually a well-rounded college applicant.

When it came time for me to apply to college, my dad said I could apply anywhere I desired and he would write the checks for my applications. "Don't worry about the cost; we'll figure it out," he told me. Though my dad reassured me that I shouldn't worry about money, I still worked to choose a school I thought we could realistically afford. I grew up going to public schools, on reduced or free lunch programs because of my parents' income, which signaled to me that my parents didn't make a lot of money. I wasn't allowed to have a job other than working for my parents at their co-owned gas station because they didn't want a job to take away from my schoolwork. The greatest expense I cost my parents was the purchase of an instrument so I could participate in the school band. In fact, because I never had my own income to depend on, conversations about money in our household sharpened my rhetorical skills—whenever we desired new clothes, a video game, or a cell phone, for instance, my brother and I drew on logos- and pathos-centered arguments to make our case for why we needed what we wanted. Anything outside of educational expenses required a strong argument. Having experienced these moments of financial stress prior to college meant that while I appreciated my dad's sentiment, I didn't want to break his bank account.

So I used my research and digital literacies to seek resources online about tuition rates at the schools that interested me. Although intrigued by Ivy League schools like Cornell or Harvard from the many glowing references to them on television, in the end I applied to only two schools—the University of Alabama, because they gave me a music scholarship and were a popular college among alumni from my high school, and the University of Mississippi, because I liked the campus when my high school class visited on a field trip. I don't regret the school I attended for my bachelor's degrees because of the memorable, rewarding, and beneficial space they gave me for my growth and learning; however, I do remember not having the heart to tell my dad of my interest in out-of-state schools once I learned of the cost. I prayed for the best, not having a clue what I was getting myself into. I was accepted to both schools on partial scholarships. Without much thought, I chose the University of Alabama, the in-state school, because of the more realistically affordable cost and closer geographical location to my family. Years ago, I promised my dad I would provide for him someday to thank him for all the things he has provided me. Though he is serious when it comes to work, my dad has a great sense of humor; whenever I bring up my plan to fund his life someday, he jokes and says he expects a check from me every month when he retires. What he may not realize is that I am being completely serious. I think about ways I could fund his retirement regularly once I gain more financial stability after graduate school.

Dressing the Part

Though I grew up working class, my values now often reflect those of middle-class academia. These shifting outlooks create tensions and conflicting understandings between my family and me. For instance, when my parents wanted to celebrate my getting into college with a gift, I asked for a North Face brand jacket.

"A jacket? We can get you a jacket. What color?" my dad asked, assuming I just wanted new clothes.

"No. Not just any jacket—a *North Face* jacket. You have to go to a special store for those, like not Walmart. They are more expensive, but they will last forever," I emphasized.

Several times my parents tried to coax me into buying another jacket, but I wouldn't budge. I desired this jacket because all of the popular students in my high school wore it—it was a status symbol. I was never one of the "popular students" or wore the fanciest clothes, and I wanted to feel what that felt like. My working-class parents don't share these material values. For them, the jacket represented a hefty price tag. But they eventually gave in and bought the jacket for a little more than $100—the most they ever spent on a single article of clothing for me. I still wear the jacket on cold days, and I thank my parents for making this valuable purchase.

Along with serving as a status symbol, the North Face jacket operated as a way to fit into my educational environment. First-generation students, or individuals who are the first in their family to graduate from college, typically come from working-class families, which often means negotiating financial challenges that contribute to "feelings of otherness" because they are working to "reconcil[e] the poverty that many had come from" while trying to "belong to the academic world" (Gardner 49). Pursuing a career in higher education involves a readapting and reconsideration of our class values. As an undergraduate, this came in the form of purchasing textbooks priced higher than any of my clothes, including my North Face jacket; on-campus housing in smaller spaces that cost as much if not more than the mortgage payments on their home; and parking passes to give me an opportunity to occupy a (not guaranteed) space. These become the necessities and luxuries of pursuing an academic degree away from home that then carried over to graduate school and beyond. In graduate school, the values of the academic middle class continued to complicate my understanding of what I *should* value. For instance, I opened a credit card account to help pay for the cost of participating in conferences, joining scholarly organizations, and reciprocating in those moments when I needed to exercise my position as an upper-level graduate student by honoring the unspoken expectation of purchasing a drink or meal for a visiting potential graduate student or colleague at a conference. I performed the middle-class values of academia by continuing to enact frugality and the skills I learned from my working-class parents, such as teaching myself how to cook well with cheaper ingredients or buying blazers secondhand. Michelle M. Tokarczyk and Elizabeth A. Fay note that women, particularly from working-class backgrounds, may feel that after earning tenured positions "they have severed all connection with their working-class backgrounds, and they have the titles and salaries to prove it. These women often display a middle-, even upper-middle class aesthetic" (6). Tokarczyk and Fay challenge the idea that one can wholly change classes, because of the values and tastes instilled in us from working-class upbringings and backgrounds; however, they wonder to what degree the "process of the doctorate dissatisf[ies] us with our backgrounds, instilling in us a desire for elite values and prejudices" (6). Fitting into a variety of class discourses while moving through the US education system requires deep reflection on our positions as working-class, first-generation teacher-scholars, but it also offers moments for us to enact our diverse class and cultural literacies to productively engage in these spaces.

The tension generated by this jacket purchase conversation perhaps came as a response to a conflation of my identity as a student with that of my parents' daughter. I never articulated to my parents why certain clothing mattered in school. I struggled to explain the significance of this particular jacket and continued to make logos-based arguments to get my parents to see this jacket as an investment in my future, much like the college acceptance that prompted its purchase. Conversations about expenses have always been complicated in our household. We talk about money, but we talk about how to save it first rather than spend it. To this day, if my mom learns the price I pay for a professional piece of clothing, better-quality lipstick, or haircut, she comments that I "must think [I'm] coming from Clinton's House and live a rich life," a reference to former President Bill Clinton and the White House, symbols of a higher class and life status.

Resisting the Good Girl

Although my parents wanted to have an educated daughter, they also wanted to raise me to be their good Indian daughter. In *Good Girls Marry Doctors*, an edited collection of essays written by and about South Asian American women about their experiences navigating, rebelling, and/or disobeying the cultural expectations of South Asian upbringings, Piyali Bhattacharya sums up the typical prospects for Good South Asian Girls, or Desi girl:

> Success is a funny thing for us Good Girls. Most of us have been schooled by our parents and communities since we were children not only to strive for but also to desire a certain kind of life: academic rigor, followed by a well-respected job, but within a career which might allow us to stay at home and raise our children once we marry a hard-working, respectful, and high-earning Desi man. [. . .] It is on the shoulders of Good Girls to carry forward cultural legacies. (vi)

As I mentioned earlier, along with gaining academic literacies, I regularly learned household literacies, ones my traditionally minded parents knew would make me a good marital candidate when my time came. My mom grew up with (and still follows) the understanding that women should serve their men, that our job is to get married, have children, and support our families. I completely disagree with my mom's perspective and began rebelling early on, arguing that women should be treated as equals and can do anything men can do. For years, my mom and I have argued whenever the topic of doing chores, especially dishes, comes up in our household. Whenever my brother offers to do dishes, he's immediately told not to worry about it and to sit down; I am expected to do dishes because I'm a woman.

Like the many South Asian women in Bhattacharya's collection, getting our education opened our eyes to feminist ideals that often make it difficult to continue to fit in with our families. An oft-noted challenge for first-generation college students is feeling "separated from their families and communities when they returned home" (Gardner & Holley 85). For me, this extends to my cultural expectations. For one, I married an American man—during the second year of my PhD program—out of love rather than accepting an arranged marriage, partially a product of growing up with American values in American society. This relationship presented many challenges for my family, who expected me to follow the arranged marriage custom. For instance, my parents dissuaded me from dating in middle and high school; we didn't talk about it. I met my husband in college; the distance from my parents allowed me to determine how I wanted to conduct my personal relationships, and telling my mom about my choice to begin dating felt less daunting over the phone.

And second, at family gatherings, other married women in my age group occasionally talk about their studies or past schooling and jobs; however, it becomes clear that they gave up these careers after marriage. While my extended family expresses pride in my pursuing a doctorate and working as a teacher, it often comes as a shock that I continue to do this even after marriage. In the midst of preparing to move to a new city and beginning my PhD program, I got engaged. Among the many expected questions that follow an engagement—When is the wedding? Where will you live after? Do you want children?—my *nani ma* (mom's mom) asked whether we would survive on my fiancé's income. Our conversation, originally in Hindi, went like this:

"We'll have my income too. I'll be in a PhD program, but I'll get paid to teach through an assistantship, like a scholarship. We'll be fine," I assured her.

"What do you mean? You can't be in school and be married. You have to stay home and take care of your husband," she said without missing a beat.

I stared at her, stunned. How could *Nani Ma* seriously think that getting engaged meant I would give up my academic goals? My mother came to the rescue.

"She's staying in school. A marriage won't disrupt her education. She can take care of him and get a PhD."

Nani Ma shook her head. "That's impossible. She has to stay at home and take care of the house and her husband. She can't do both. She won't have time."

I knew my choice to break with my family's tradition of arranged marriage, especially with a White, American man, would create challenges for my *nani ma*, who came from a more traditional Indian upbringing than my mom; yet I found myself speechless at the notion that I couldn't pursue my education and marriage at the same time. I felt frustrated also by my mom's response, expecting me to "take care of" my future husband. Taking me aside, my mom told me that I needed to remember that *Nani Ma* grew up in a more conservative country and that, around her, I might need to mention my studies less in conversation and focus more on my household activities. So around *Nani Ma*, I more actively take on household duties such as cooking and cleaning to keep her respect. These rhetorical choices to suppress my feminist values for my family act like a set of masks—or aprons, in this case—that I wear at home, similar to the masks many scholars wear when navigating "imposter syndrome" or "feeling[s] that one's ability is not sufficient to warrant one's position" in academia (Hamilton 2–3; see also Okawa; Kniffin; Gardner and Holley; Boehm and Lueck). Traditional dress, oven mitts, and wedding jewelry function rhetorically as parts of my "good Indian American daughter" persona, just as cardigans and dress pants enact my "teacher" persona.

Rewriting the (Single) Story

My father's interest in a "better life" for me and my brother included us getting college degrees so that we would have mobility in the American job landscape. He didn't want us to endure jobs that required heavy physical labor like those he continued to work in. Because of my success in humanities and arts-oriented classes and my love of the movie *The Devil Wears Prada* throughout high school, I pursued two writing-and-language-focused bachelor's degrees as an undergraduate: an English degree with a minor in Italian and a journalism degree with a minor in music. These early degrees required me to take numerous writing classes and engage in research, learn interview methods, and write in many different genres, all of which I now practice in my daily work in rhetoric and composition.

My journey into rhetoric and composition began during my junior year, when I first heard about the field from Erin T. Chandler, who was working on her doctorate in rhetoric and composition at the time at the University of Alabama. In her Technical Writing class, Professor Chandler tasked us with creating mock job and graduate program application portfolios. While the genre of a job portfolio seemed relatively straightforward, the graduate school personal statement eluded me. I framed my mock statement around what I felt appealed to a graduate program in literature. In her feedback, Professor Chandler noted that the field of rhetoric and composition better fit what I described in my materials. *There's a field that studies writing like this?* I pondered excitedly as I read through articles she provided me as a way to briefly orient me to the field.

Less than a year later, when it came time for me to apply to graduate programs, Professor Amy Dayton sent me Amy Tan's "Mother Tongue" in response to frustration I expressed in a reading response about standardized testing as a multilingual student. In an email response, I described how I had never felt such a connection to a piece of writing as I did to Tan's essay: "I felt like Amy Tan was in fact, *Ashanka Kumari*," I wrote at the time to begin to describe the similarities between Tan's story and my own. In the opening of her essay, Tan writes that she is "not a scholar of English or literature," but instead "a writer. And by that definition, I am someone who has always loved language" (7). Tan's description of her multilingual upbringing and relationship with her mother mirrors much of my own, similar to how Sergio Figueiredo felt about understanding his family's communication practices after reading scholarship by Eric Havelock, Walter Ong, and Gregory Ulmer (this volume). Reading Tan was the first time I saw the real potential for me to have a career as a writer and researcher who studies language practices. I bring up these two brief anecdotes because they explain my choice to pursue a career in rhetoric and composition, one I understood and continue to see as valuing language and cultural diversity in writing practices. Before my orientation to the field, I struggled to find my footing, and felt that, if I wanted my writing to make an impact, I needed to write like the many White, male, often British authors I read in my literature classes or whose journalism was praised in my journalism courses. Instead, I discovered a discipline that felt like a more logical fit for my desire to both write and teach writing.

I remember when I got accepted to the University of Nebraska–Lincoln, where I ultimately got my master's in composition and rhetoric. As the first program to send me an acceptance letter, I recognized it as a big deal on its own since I wasn't sure I would get in anywhere—I had applied to thirteen programs for my MA for fear of not getting accepted somewhere. I didn't have the best GRE scores, and while my GPA was good, it could always be better. I doubted myself and my work despite the support of many teacher-mentors and my family. I called my dad moments after hearing the voice mail about my acceptance with funding.

"So, you're moving to Nebraska?" he asked.

"Not exactly. I need to wait to hear from the other twelve schools I applied to. It isn't that simple," I tried to explain.

"When do you want to visit Nebraska?"

Over the next few weeks, phone calls with my dad consisted of grand visions of my imagined move to Nebraska. He mapped out the distance between Nebraska and my parents, from family friends, from Canada where my aunt lived. He offered suggestions for how I could break up the monthly stipend to live and eat. All things considered, Nebraska was a long way away from everything. To put it into perspective, I had lived no less than three hours away from my parents my entire life. With the exception of a few months I spent in Europe for a study abroad program (Italy) and an internship (Spain) during summers in my undergraduate program, I had never resided too far from my family.

When I told my parents I wanted to continue on to graduate programs rather than move straight into a job, they were supportive. We all worried about the cost of graduate school, but once I learned about assistantships and stipends from professors who mentored me through the application process, my family became more at ease. Uncertainty around the purpose of graduate school and higher education meant a renegotiation of my parents' and my own understanding of career goals. While I had fulfilled my dad's main life goal for me, I then became the person who "wanted better," and created a new path for myself beyond my family's expectations. My parents didn't know what to make of my master's education, though I tried to explain it as well as I understood it. Now I've learned to speak vaguely about what I do in graduate school and in academia: I write. I teach. I read. Lather, rinse, repeat. These are the terms my parents understand about the work I do, which they do not see as *work* since it isn't some kind of physical labor; they categorize it as *studying* or *learning* or *teaching*.

This negotiation continued in my pursuit of the PhD at the University of Louisville. I chose not only a location that was closer to my family in Alabama, but also a research path that continued to place my background and family at the forefront of my work—I wrote about first-generation-to-college doctoral students in rhetoric and composition for my dissertation, among other projects. I engage in identity and literacy studies across all of my work, regularly reflecting on my own changing identity and notions of performance across spaces. Additionally, my pedagogy takes a pop culture approach as influenced by the impact of pop culture on my own upbringing. I attribute much of my success both to the life my immigrant parents gave me and to my first-generation student status, and engage excitedly in all of my academic and personal pursuits to carry forward my parents' legacy and my redefined ambition for a "better" life.

Meanwhile, I continue to serve as my parents' go-to language broker, especially given my now advanced knowledge in English studies. Just as I teach my students to engage with iMovie and the Purdue OWL, I teach my parents how to use their computers, smartphones, and printers—I spend these interactions thinking about my students' and my parents' literacies, particularly digital literacies. I regularly receive phone calls asking for help filling out forms. During my master's program, my mom began her pursuit of American citizenship. I would call her regularly and quiz her on the questions she would be asked while breaking down concepts like the right to bear arms or the role of senators. I approach working with my parents similarly to the way I work with students in the writing classroom: with patience, openness, and energy as they learn new concepts.

Ever since I started college at Alabama, I have tried to call my dad regularly each week. He's usually at work or on his lunch break. Normally I'm greeted by an excited "Hello, *Didi!*" Though I'm his *beta,* his daughter, my dad more often calls me his *didi,* his sister. Even my brother doesn't call me *Didi* anymore and refers to me by my first name. My dad has only one real sister, but she passed away during my last year of undergrad. I don't think I've ever heard him call his sisters-in-law *Didi*; he calls me *Didi* like a younger brother would call his older sister, out of respect. This deep relationship inevitably develops between many first-generation immigrant children and their parents, especially as language brokers for their families. We engage in a reciprocal dependency from love that complicates Brandt's notion of sponsorship—I depend on my parents to help financially and emotionally support me through my education through their often physical labor, as they depend on me to support them through navigating America; together, we grow and learn from one another about the possibilities of living as Indian Americans. If my dad is at work when I call him, I hear cash register noises.

"Hello?"

"Hello!"

"Hello, *Didi*! Hello . . . How are you? . . . That be all?"

"I'm good. How are you?"

"Pump 4? OK. Good, good."—*Ka-ching*—"Thank you, have a good day. What are you doing? Hello, sir! That be all?"

"I'm walking to school as usual. It's a nice day here."

"Walking to school? Hello."—*Ka-ching*—"Good. It's OK here. Raining a little. Thank you, have a good day. Hello."

My dad speaks in fragments, but I've mastered his rhythm. He speaks in broken English, but that's just part of his charm.

No matter how busy he is, he will always attempt to speak with me when I call. No matter what we talk about, our conversations end the same way.

"I love you, *Beta*."

"I love you too, Daddy."

"Be careful."

Works Cited

Adichie, Chimamanda Ngozi. "The Danger of a Single Story." *TED*, July 2009, https://www.ted.com/talks/chimamanda_adichie_the_danger_of_a_single_story.

Alvarez, Steven. "Brokering Literacies: Child Language Brokering in Mexican Immigrant Families." *Community Literacy Journal*, vol. 11, no. 2, 2017, pp. 1–15.

Bhattacharya, Piyali, editor. *Good Girls Marry Doctors: South Asian American Daughters on Obedience and Rebellion*. Aunt Lute Books, 2016.

Boehm, Beth, and Amy J. Lueck. "Graduate Student Peer Mentoring Programs: Benefitting Students, Faculty and Academic Programs." *The Mentoring Continuum: From Graduate School through Tenure*, edited by Glenn Wright, Syracuse UP, 2016, pp. 187–202.

Bourdieu, Pierre. *Distinction: A Social Critique of the Judgement of Taste*. Harvard UP, 1984.

Brandt, Deborah. "Sponsors of Literacy." *College Composition and Communication*, vol. 49, no. 2, 1998, pp. 165–85, http://www.jstor.org/stable/358929.

Ganti, Tejaswini. *Bollywood: A Guidebook to Popular Hindi Cinema*. Routledge, 2004.

Gardner, Susan K. "The Challenges of First-Generation Doctoral Students." *New Directions for Higher Education*, no. 163, 2013, pp. 43–54, doi:10.1002/he.

Gardner, Susan K., and Karri A. Holley. "'Those Invisible Barriers Are Real': The Progression of First-Generation Students through Doctoral Education." *Equity & Excellence in Education*, vol. 44, no. 1, 2011, pp. 77–92.

Hamilton, Sharon Jean. *My Name's Not Susie: A Life Transformed by Literacy.* Boynton/Cook, 1995.

Kniffin, Kevin M. "Accessibility to the PhD and Professoriate for First-Generation College Graduates: Review and Implications for Students, Faculty, and Campus Policies." *American Academic*, vol. 3, 2007, pp. 49–80.

Moss, Beverly J. "Intersections of Race and Class in the Academy." *Coming to Class: Pedagogy and the Social Class of Teachers*, edited by Alan Shepard et al., Boynton/Cook, 1998, pp. 157–69.

Okawa, Gail Y. "Diving for Pearls: Mentoring as Cultural and Activist Practice among Academics of Color." *College Composition and Communication*, vol. 53, no. 3, 2002, pp. 507–32.

Tan, Amy. "Mother Tongue." *The Threepenny Review*, no. 43, 1990, pp. 7–8.

Tokarczyk, Michelle M., and Elizabeth A. Fay, editors. *Working-Class Women in the Academy: Laborers in the Knowledge Factory.* U of Massachusetts P, 1993.

CHAPTER FOUR

Writing to Name: Documents, Movement, and Disruptions of a New Filipino Immigrant Teacher-Scholar

PETER MAYSHLE
Carnegie Mellon University

"I have signed my name," said Louis, "already twenty times. I, and again I, and again I. Clear, firm, unequivocal, there it stands, my name. Clear-cut and unequivocal am I too."

—VIRGINIA WOOLF, *The Waves*

[T]he boundary becomes the place from which something begins its presencing in a movement not dissimilar to the ambulant, ambivalent articulation of the beyond that I have drawn out: "Always and ever differently the bridge escorts the lingering and hastening ways of men to and fro, so that they may get to other banks.... The bridge gathers as a passage that crosses."

—HOMI K. BHABHA, *The Location of Culture*

Two things occurred in 2015 that sparked the writing of this essay: first, happy that I'd landed a job right after graduation last year, a friend of mine, who teaches at a huge public university in New Jersey, advised that I should also use my middle name to signal my ethnicity/difference. Instead of "Peter Mayshle," he explained, I should be using "Peter *Zaragoza* Mayshle," the assumption being that "Zaragoza" announces my Other-ness, thereby marking me as a potential ally or mentor for students of color on campus. My friend's advice was well considered: I was teaching in a small city in upstate New York, where the population is predominately White, at a small private liberal arts college, where 60 percent of the student body comes from New York and New England, and whose families boast a median income upwards of $140,000.

Second, as I began preparing the papers for my application for permanent residency the following summer, I was confronted by the name on my birth certificate (see Figure 4.1), a key requirement of the application. On it, it says my first name is "George," but I've gone by the name "Peter" ever since I was a little boy. And on all of my official documents—as much as I can gather and as far as I can remember—my name has always been "Peter George." My truncated first name on my birth certificate now needed to be corrected, a process that normally takes up to three months working with the local civil registry in Manila, Philippines, where I'm from.

These two incidents foreground the importance of names or the act of naming, and all of the complicated tensions associated with it, including those that speak toward marking a person of color's identity in the United States. But I'm not just a person of color; I am also, perhaps more so, a nonnative, an "international." I grew up in the Philippines, where the majority of my undergraduate education was taught in English. I graduated with an MFA from a creative writing program in Ann Arbor, Michigan, and a doctorate degree in English from a composition and rhetoric program in Madison, Wisconsin. (A tropical island boy in snow-blasted landscapes, I used to say.) My dissertation was on spatial rhetorics and public memory. In my first year of teaching, I taught three first-year composition courses, a 200-level travel writing course, and an upper-level course on the rhetoric of place. In the fall of that year, I taught the first upper-level course on the rhetoric of memory on campus. I consider myself a rhetoric scholar who also teaches composition, and I use the name "Peter Mayshle."

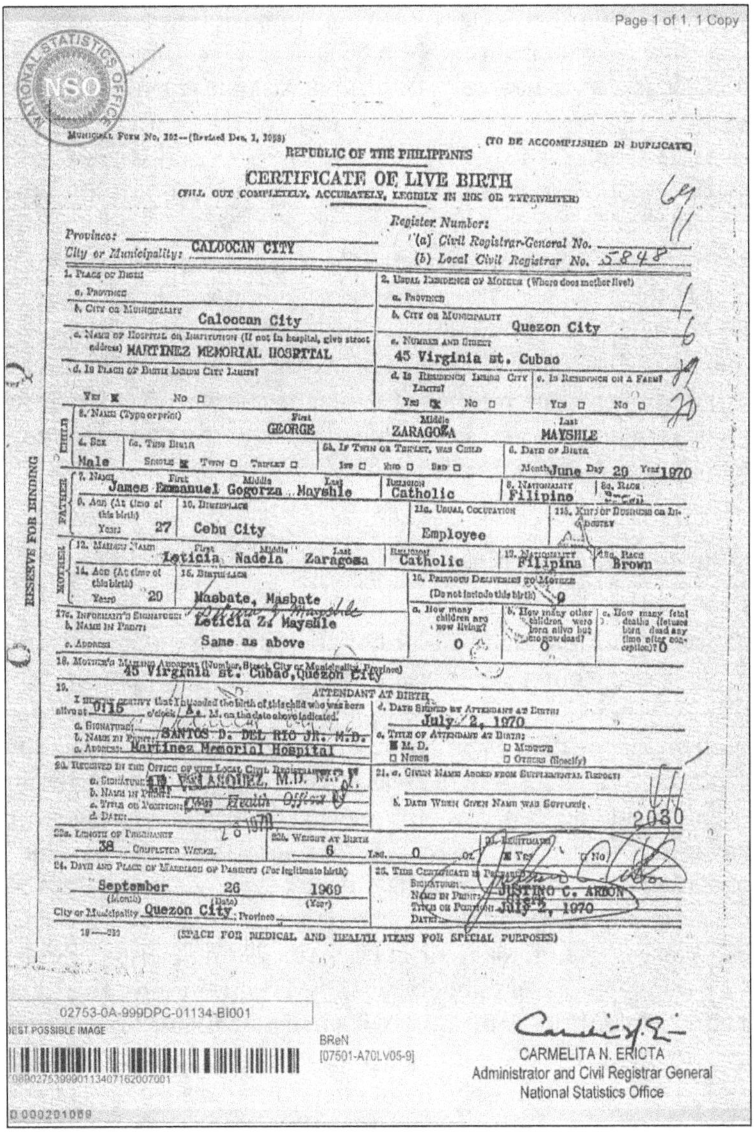

Page 1 of 1, 1 Copy

NATIONAL STATISTICS OFFICE NSO

Municipal Form No. 102—(Revised Dec. 1, 1958)

(TO BE ACCOMPLISHED IN DUPLICATE)

REPUBLIC OF THE PHILIPPINES

CERTIFICATE OF LIVE BIRTH

(FILL OUT COMPLETELY, ACCURATELY, LEGIBLY IN INK OR TYPEWRITER)

Province:

City or Municipality: CALOOCAN CITY

Register Number:

(a) Civil Registrar-General No.

(b) Local Civil Registrar No. 5848

1. Place of Birth
a. Province
b. City or Municipality: Caloocan City
c. Name of Hospital or Institution (If not in hospital, give street address): MARTINEZ MEMORIAL HOSPITAL
d. Is Place of Birth Inside City Limits? Yes ☒ No ☐

2. Usual Residence of Mother (Where does mother live?)
a. Province
b. City or Municipality: Quezon City
c. Number and Street: 45 Virginia st. Cubao
d. Is Residence Inside City Limits? Yes ☒ No ☐
e. Is Residence on a Farm? Yes ☐ No ☐

CHILD

3. Name (Type or print) — First: GEORGE — Middle: ZARAGOZA — Last: MAYSHLE

4. Sex: Male

5a. This Birth: Single ☒ Twin ☐ Triplet ☐

5b. If Twin or Triplet, was Child: 1st ☐ 2nd ☐ 3rd ☐

6. Date of Birth: Month June Day 20 Year 1970

FATHER

7. Name — First: James Emmanuel — Middle: Gogorza — Last: Mayshle

Religion: Catholic

8. Nationality: Filipino

8a. Race: Brown

9. Age (At time of this birth): 27 Years

10. Birthplace: Cebu City

11a. Usual Occupation: Employee

11b. Kind of Business or Industry

MOTHER

12. Maiden Name — First: Leticia — Middle: Nadela — Last: Zaragosa

Religion: Catholic

13. Nationality: Filipina

13a. Race: Brown

14. Age (At time of this birth): 20 Years

15. Birthplace: Masbate, Masbate

16. Previous Deliveries to Mother (Do not include this birth)
a. How many children are now living? 0
b. How many other children were born alive but are now dead? 0
c. How many fetal deaths (fetuses born dead any time after conception)? 0

17a. Informant's Signature:
b. Name in Print: Leticia Z. Mayshle
c. Address: Same as above

18. Mother's Mailing Address (Number, Street, City or Municipality, Province): 45 Virginia st. Cubao, Quezon City

19. ATTENDANT AT BIRTH

I hereby certify that I attended the birth of this child who was born alive at 0115 o'clock A. M. on the date above indicated.
a. Signature:
b. Name in Print: SANTOS D. DEL RIO JR. M.D.
c. Address: Martinez Memorial Hospital

d. Date Signed by Attendant at Birth: July 2, 1970

e. Title of Attendant at Birth: ☒ M.D. ☐ Midwife ☐ Nurse ☐ Others (Specify)

20. Received in the Office of the Local Civil Registrar
a. Signature:
b. Name in Print: VELASQUEZ, M.D.
c. Title or Position: City Health Officer
d. Date:

21. a. Given Name Added from Supplemental Report:
b. Date When Given Name was Supplied:

2080

22a. Length of Pregnancy: 38 Completed Weeks

22b. Weight at Birth: 6 Lbs. 0 Oz.

23. Legitimate? ☒ Yes ☐ No

24. Date and Place of Marriage of Parents (For legitimate birth): September 26 1969 (Month) (Date) (Year)
City or Municipality: Quezon City; Province

25. This Certificate is Prepared by:
Signature:
Name in Print: JUSTINO C. ARBON
Title or Position: Clerk
Date: July 2, 1970

(SPACE FOR MEDICAL AND HEALTH ITEMS FOR SPECIAL PURPOSES)

02753-0A-999DPC-01134-BI001

BEST POSSIBLE IMAGE

BReN
[07501-A70LV05-9]

CARMELITA N. ERICTA
Administrator and Civil Registrar General
National Statistics Office

0 000201089

FIGURE 4.1. *The author's birth certificate.*

Pierre Bourdieu's claim that the "imposition of a name . . . is to *signify* to someone what he is and how he should conduct himself as a consequence" (120, emphasis in original) is relevant to me in this essay: What does it mean, for the composition and rhetoric scholar, to signify, to *name oneself*? And what does it mean for one's students? As I hope to show, contrary to what Woolf's Louis expresses in the chapter epigraph, naming can never be "clear-cut" or "unequivocal." As a beginning scholar who is also in the process of transitioning as an immigrant, the issue of my name and the power of naming began for me long before I moved to this country. The questions that these experiences had brought up for me proceeded to haunt me when I started my graduate education here in the United States and are now foremost in my mind as a new teacher-scholar.

What's in a (My) Name?

My relationship with my name has always had a fraught history. From a very young age, I was taught to write my name in full, that is, "Peter George Zaragoza Mayshle." "Peter" because I was born on the feast day of St. Peter. Growing up in a predominantly Catholic country, this name was inevitable. My grandfather insisted on adding "George" for reasons that no one now knows anymore. "Zaragoza" is my mother's surname and "Mayshle" my father's. I trace my Spanish heritage not to "Zaragoza" but to my mestiza grandmother, Remedios Gogorza, on my father's side.

Moreover, not apparent in my name is my Jewish heritage, very small but present nonetheless. ("Mayshle" is an Americanized version of the Austrian-Jewish name "Mischle," my great-grandfather Joseph. According to one of his granddaughters, great *lolo* Joseph landed in Cebu with other Europeans as they fled the Nazi persecution before World War II.)

Of course, this multiplicity of heritage is not unique to me; I am not unlike other Filipinos who trace their family heritage through a turbid haze of "Third World" history. Four hundred years of combined colonization (300 years by Spain and then 50 years by the United States), conflated by 4 years of Japanese invasion and centuries of Chinese assimilation, have transformed the Philippines into a nation of mixed-heritage citizens. Filipino names, therefore, become emblematic of the country's historical portrait of invasions, colonizations, creolizations, intermarriages, and modern global exchanges. I see my name as evidence of my Malay, Spanish, Jewish, and European backgrounds. In short, I see my name as very Filipino, emblematic of Filipino history and culture.

My earliest official documents only served to mark additional layers of complication, if you will. While my birth certificate, as I've already mentioned, lacks one first name, my baptismal certificate (see Figure 4.2) generously provides me with three, "Peter Paul George," as the priest performing the baptism not-so-sternly reminded my parents and grandparents that my birthdate is also the feast day of St. Paul. My baby book (see Figure 4.3), filled out in my mother's handwriting, and one of my first school ID cards (see Figure 4.4), both carry my complete first name with my middle name "Zaragoza" expunged (much to the chagrin of my first-grade self, apparently).

Growing up, I thought I'd ignore these documents and simplify matters by just sticking to "Peter Mayshle." I soon realized that this didn't really help much, as my personal encounters both in school and, later on, at work included my addressing two questions frequently posed to me: *How do you pronounce your last name?* and *How do you spell it?* There are very few Mayshles in the Philippines, and the Americanized Jewish name can be difficult for anyone to spell, so these questions never really bothered me; I was only too happy to provide the information, proud that my name was unique and piqued the interest of strangers. But when I moved to the United States, these two questions were now followed almost always by a third: *What's your background?* Or more often: *Where are you from originally?* Of course, I would always answer that I'm from the Philippines and/or I'm Filipino, and the first few times it happened, it wasn't a big deal. But the more I was asked that question and the more I engaged with the person asking the question, the more I realized it was the truest question of the three—meaning, it was *the* question that the other person *really* wanted answered, and that the person asking it wasn't only making an explicit act of seeking information; the person was also making, intentionally or not, an implicit gesture

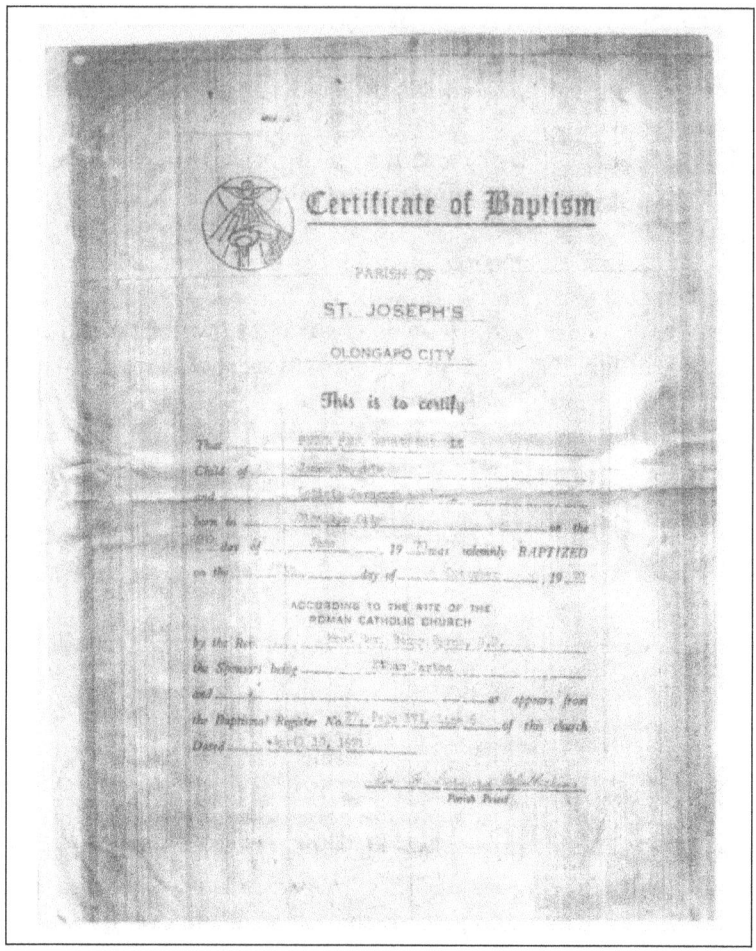

FIGURE 4.2. *The author's baptismal certificate.*

of rendering judgment. The judgment being that I'm clearly not from the United States.

In other words, I became Filipino the moment I moved here. What I mean by this is that having lived most of my life in the Philippines, I've never had to declare myself as Filipino. I knew who I was—Filipino, like everyone else—and I just went about my days, living my middle-class working life, unchallenged, unquestioning. In the Philippines, I was at the center; I became an

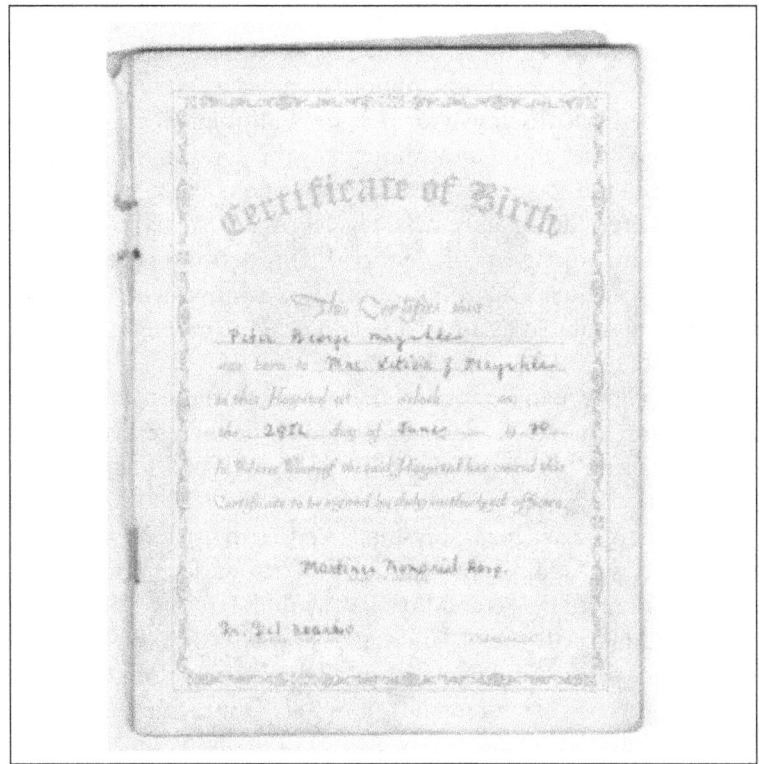

FIGURE 4.3. *The author's baby book.*

FIGURE 4.4. *The author's grade 1 ID.*

Other the moment I moved away from that center. Here in the States, I instantly, simply by moving here, became a minority. In this way, my becoming a minority begins as an act of "naming"—whether consciously or not, by willful intent or innocent mistake—thrust upon the minority subject by the dominant members of the society. I never saw myself as "Filipino" before I moved to the United States, where issues of race, sexuality, gender, class, and other markers of identity thickly permeate every social situation in which I now find myself. I was now, whether I like it or not, designated as a person of color. One moment I wasn't, the next I just was.

When I began my graduate education here in the United States a little more than a decade ago, I made a deliberate decision to continue using "Peter Mayshle," even though my official documents (my passport, my F-1 student visa, and I-20) say that I'm "Peter George Zaragoza Mayshle." And I still use it now. Part of the reason was again for simplicity's sake, but deep down I also felt that the name "Peter Mayshle" would ease my adjustment into the American social landscape, particularly the American classroom. Many Americans, after all, have simple Anglo-Saxon names composed of a forename followed by a surname, and "Peter Mayshle" fits that bill perfectly. Also, I thought "Peter Mayshle" looked and sounded, well, *American*. In a way, I thought the name would make me belong because it would render me invisible. If I use "Peter *Zaragoza* Mayshle," as my friend advised, I would announce my difference—and thereby separate myself from the majority. But I don't want to be separate. I don't want to be different.

Or rather, I want to be different *and* I want to belong. I want to retain my heritage while simultaneously immersing myself in a new adopted homeland.

Naming the Minority

Scholars from various disciplines recognize naming as a highly political act, one that can empower, sustain, or disenfranchise (Chan; Hayakawa and Hayakawa; Maulucci and Mensah; Solórzano and Yosso). As Maulucci and Mensah note:

> Terms such as minority, non-dominant, and non-White . . . carry judgments that position people as inferior. The term non-White categorizes people based on what or who they are not; it is a term of exclusion, and it reinforces the idea that White is the normative racial standard against which all other races should be measured. (2)

Therefore, one must be careful with the words one uses, particularly because words not only carry information but also impart judgment. This tension between exclusion and inclusion that I feel when my background is queried may be triggered by a curiosity over my name, but it is certainly undergirded by an assessment of my minority subject position.

In other words, names are only part of the issue. Naming intersects not just with national and racial categories but also with other identity markers such as gender, sexuality, religion, disability status, and class. Our names are recorded not just on written documents; they are embodied characteristics of our being in the world. Part of these embodied characteristics encompass our language use, and scholars have observed that our relationship to language—whether to our first, native language or to a second, adopted one—becomes either a useful tool or a burdensome hindrance in our engagement with our social environments (de los Reyes; Kovalyova; Guglielmo in this volume). We "name" ourselves and one another by our bodies and by the actions our bodies perform, the gestures our bodies enact, the speeches our bodies utter.

For the minority subject, naming becomes all the more crucial in moments when the tension between exclusion and inclusion becomes more acutely felt. As postcolonial critic Homi Bhabha notes:

> Terms of cultural engagement, whether antagonistic or affiliative, are produced performatively. The representation of difference must not be hastily read as the reflection of pre-given ethnic or cultural traits set in the fixed tablet of tradition. The social articulation of difference, from the minority perspective, is a complex, on-going negotiation that seeks to authorize cultural hybridities that emerge in moments of historical transformation. (2)

Now, as a minority subject, I find myself performing that "complex, on-going negotiation" of having to unpack the various meanings and implications of this newly acquired subject position, consciously having to explain myself to myself first before being able to explain myself to the dominant culture. For example, should I pursue my position as *Filipino*, a complete foreigner in an alien culture, the outsider looking in? Or should I self-identify as a *Filipino American* (a position I'm not so comfortable taking, at least not yet) so that I may join one of the largest and most resilient of Asian American communities? If not Filipino American, is there a middle ground, a sort of "transition" identity, one that will move from alien subject to native? Maybe this is what Raymond Williams is referring to when he speaks of "pre-emergent" discourse, one that is "active and pressing but not yet fully articulated" (126). Do I accept the name "minority"?

Perhaps it's not really so much about identity as it is about relationships to a place and history. In the Philippines, I'm considered middle class and the empowered majority. Here in the United States, I am a former colonial subject who is now an overseas Filipino working professionally. It seems that *I* didn't really change, just my context, which is now changing me.

Maybe the question shouldn't be *who* am I. Maybe the question should be *where* am I, or even *when* am I. *Where am I* when the head of the ESL program at the midwestern public university where I did my doctoral work got in touch before I flew out to the United States and conducted a conversation with me over the phone in order to make sure that I spoke English clearly? After about ten minutes, she sheepishly gave me her blessing when she couldn't detect anything wrong with the way I spoke, and even complimented me on my absence of an accent, which to her ear actually sounded very midwestern. My advisor, of course, apologized profusely for this incident, explaining that it is one of those embarrassing requirements imposed by the university on foreign students, especially international graduate students awarded teaching assistantships. Apparently, teaching in clear, intelligible English—ideally absent of any accent—is the imperative in American education. *Where am I* when, as a new teaching assistant, I was approached by one of my students who wanted to know if I had grown up in the United States? He was asking because he's married to a Filipino American woman and, according to him, she's never spoken English as well as I do. *Where and when am I* when I Skype weekly with my friends and family back home? Over flickering screens and crackling audio—due to the unreliable digital services in the Philippines—we share stories and update one another about our lives, all over a time difference of twelve hours. These experiences and more have blurred the boundaries of "home" and "away," "native" and "nonnative" for me in significant ways. Like never before, space and time have exerted a powerful sway over who I am and who I will be.

For example, I now know that this dialectic of inclusion and exclusion has largely informed my persona here in the United States, both within and outside of academe. Brown, middle-aged, bespectacled, and sporting thinning, graying hair, I am uncomfortable in my clothing, awkward in my comportment when I deal with White Americans. I may speak and write relatively correct and fluent English, but I am always conscious of my limitations, especially with regard to colloquial language. I sometimes stutter over certain words when in the company of native English speakers, which is almost always when I'm in the United States. I am also less funny, realizing that my kind of humor doesn't translate well from my very Filipino frames of reference, and yet I understand quite well every nuance of many American jokes. Moreover, I become most anxious during public presentations, especially at academic conferences. Wanting to be accepted into the community of my scholarly peers, I am very dependent on my printed-out, marked-up paper, finding assurance and comfort in the reading of words on the page before an audience; Q&A, for me, becomes a veritable landmine of faltering responses and half- answers, fearful that I'll be found out as nothing more than a pretender, a fake. As I recall the various conferences I've attended, I envy those academics who can project such imposing authority, sometimes even presenting their papers sans the actual papers before them, performing with admirable, seemingly extempore, confidence. As a scholar of rhetoric, surely I should be able to look the part, speak eloquently, and converse profoundly with my peers on the most pressing questions in our field. Perhaps for minority scholars, this self-consciousness becomes more acutely felt during such a threshold moment—and a conference presentation is definitely such a moment—when they must prove themselves in the glare of an audience weighing their every word, measuring their every thought. I find the stakes, at least for me, to be much higher when the context must match the content, when the performance must illuminate the script.

What I'm describing could certainly be attributed to impostor syndrome, a feeling common in academia, and all too commonly felt by "women, people of color, and first generation students" (Herrmann par. 3). Defined as "deep feelings of intellectual and professional phoniness" (Dancy and Brown 616), the impostor syndrome is socially and systemically produced. As one researcher describes it, gender- and race-based discrimination persist, so it's no wonder that researchers "who are not white, male, and middle-class might feel that they are 'faking it' and will eventually be caught out by smarter (read: white, male, and middle-class) colleagues" (Thompson par. 13). But I believe there's more than just the impostor syndrome at work here.

Compounding all this, of course, is my being a nonnative as well. ("The impostor is also *not a citizen!*") Part of the problem surely stems from my now being caught in this web of multiple subject positions—as Filipino, as foreign worker, as minority subject, as academic colleague, as teacher of composition and rhetoric, and as writer, as well as all of their various intersecting permutations. This state of being is part and parcel of the *in-between*, Bhabha's term for describing the liminal condition of hybrid subjects. Being in-between is a fraught space, a "terrain for elaborating strategies of selfhood— singular or communal—that initiate new signs of identity, and innovative sites of collaboration, and contestation, in the act of defining the idea of society itself" (Bhabha 4). The question, therefore, becomes: How does one effectively navigate this precarious space?

A promising answer, I believe, lies in the examples of two feminist critics of Asian descent: literary and cultural critic Gayatri Chakravorty Spivak and documentary filmmaker, ethnographer, and cultural theorist Trinh T. Minh-ha. In rhetoric scholar Susan C. Jarratt's reading of these scholars, she sees two fleet-footed practices of self-representation. Examining Spivak's now-canonical essay "Can the Subaltern Speak?" and her series of interviews collected in *The Post-Colonial Critic*, Jarratt finds that Spivak refuses several options for self-representation. Instead, Spivak chooses to practice what she calls *deidentification*, which is "a claiming of an identity from a text that comes from somewhere else" (qtd. in Jarratt 116). It is a process of "contexture and displacement" that begins with identifying herself with "contingent and polemical labels—'woman,' 'literary critic,' 'Asian intellectual,' 'Non-Resident Indian'" (Jarratt 116), and then continues with "a reactive strategy, adopting different identities at different times to create a consciousness of the hazards of fixity and substitution" (Jarratt 117). Spivak seems to be saying: "If you take me to be a feminist, I'll show you how I'm not the same as Western feminists. If you take me for an Indian, I'll explain elite immigrant privilege. If you define me as anti-institutional, I'll show you the disciplinarian. Spivak consistently cannot be found where she is sought" (Jarratt 117). By *periodizing*—that is, specifying the geographic, economic, and class locations of her background and academic formation—Spivak is "connecting academic practices with modes of production and larger historical movements, rather than assuming their distance from the material world" (Ahmad qtd. in Jarratt 117).

On the other hand, Trinh T. Minh-ha, in *Woman, Native, Other: Writing Postcoloniality and Feminism*," constructs a self that is "figured by the broken mirror" and "dispersed throughout her text" (Jarratt 119). This self that Minh-ha creates does not cease reflecting: "[H]ere reality is not reconstituted, it is put into pieces so as to allow another world to rebuild itself with its debris" (qtd. in Jarratt 119). Jarratt also observes that Minh-ha seems to revel in the multiplicity of voices in her writing, as she divides herself into subject and object through a play of pronouns: "[W]riting [...] is an ongoing practice that is concerned not with inserting a 'me' into language, but with creating an opening where the 'me' disappears while 'I' endlessly come and go" (qtd. in Jarratt 119). In this sense, Minh-ha and Spivak seem to use similar tactics in their adroit deflecting of any attempts at essentializing. But Minh-ha is more at ease than Spivak "in making common cause across differences," and the "radical dispersion of [Minh-ha's] self through writing coexists in [her] text with a voice of collective solidarity" (Jarratt 120). As Minh-ha writes: "The process of differentiation [...] continues, and speaking nearby or together with certainly differs from speaking for and about," and "[d]ifference does not annul identity. It is beyond and alongside identity" (qtd. in Jarratt 121).

Reading about these two feminist scholars, I find their nimble tactics of self-representation useful for my ongoing struggle with naming myself to myself and others. I am drawn to the very practical rhetoric they deploy to suit their varied multiple locations. It's true that they are very much aware of their representational function, that they *do* speak for the Other, but they also "simultaneously recast images and frustrate any simple process of representation. As postcolonial subjects located in the metropolitan academic scene, both choose a complex construction of subjectivity in an ethical response to the exigencies of that placement" (Jarratt 121).

Following Spivak's and Minh-ha's examples, I need to resist the binary categories of "native" and "nonnative" or "citizen" and "alien" and enact productive, critical practices that acknowledge mixed and multiple subjectivities. Perhaps instead of positionality, I should start thinking in terms of *motionality*, whereby belonging is formed not so much by strict adherence to official hegemonic structures but by movement along and between always shifting borders of belonging.

Motion or movement informs Jenny Edbauer's concept of distributed rhetorical ecologies. Seeing rhetoric as movement underscores the value of viewing "counter-rhetorics, issues of cooptation, and strategies of rhetorical production and circulation . . . [so that] we can begin to recognize the way rhetorics are held together trans-situationally, as well as the effects of trans-situationality on rhetorical circulation" (20).

Seeing rhetoric as movement helps us see identity as a process, an ongoing negotiation. Yes, this impostor is not a citizen, but instead is a *citizen in the making*, a dynamic conception "which not only acknowledges but makes productive use of the flux and fluidity of language, culture and identity in everyday life" (Guerra 100). This is what the recent turn to the concept of translanguaging or translingualism means:

> Each of us not only possesses a multiplicity of linguistically and culturally-accented identities; we also invoke hybrid, or what I

prefer to call translingual/transcultural, identities as we move across the varied communities of belonging that we occupy at any given moment and that are themselves continuously changing. (Guerra 100)

Therefore, for me, moving along and between borders requires the *continual* practice of disruption, which entails questioning accepted assumptions, looking critically at how stereotypes are formed and disseminated, and resisting the labels and social markers that brand one as the Other. Motionality and disruption recognize that there is no center, or rather, the center can be anyone and everyone.

Writing to Name

Looking again at all the documents I've gathered around me in order to write this chapter—my birth certificate, school IDs, report cards, I-20s, and other official or institutional documents—I have come to this conclusion: We are named by the documents that identify us, but we can also name ourselves by the documents we create. In my case, my writing this essay becomes my way of naming myself to myself and to you, the reader. This is what I mean by the phrase "writing to name": I write to name myself as a scholar, as a teacher, as a writer. And it is an ongoing process, not *to name* as a finished act, but *to keep writing, to keep naming*. For my students, it means writing to name themselves continuously as rigorous, critical thinkers who can engage with the community within the academy and beyond. Echoing bell hooks's "coming to voice," writing to name is a highly disruptive but transformative act. This disruption that I speak of becomes all the more imperative to me as a teacher of composition and rhetoric when I work with young students whose voices are still developing and whose identities are still forming. It may seem counterintuitive to disrupt their already tumultuous young lives and throw them further into chaos at such a tender time in their intellectual development, but the goal of teaching shouldn't be inculcating fixed knowledge and calcifying widely held beliefs; it should be about unsettling assumptions with laser-critical lenses.

Writing to name in the classroom begins with my teaching persona, which is very much informed by my being Filipino, my being foreign, and the authority (or sense of it) I create and wield in the classroom is inextricably tied to that. My foreignness is noticeable; I cannot hide it. So I address it first thing in class, to gain my students' trust, to assure them that I am a competent instructor. I say that I come from the Philippines, new to their country, though I've been living here on and off for more than ten years now, and I have been writing most of my life. I tell them about my advertising background, my graduate education, my research, and some of my publications. This may be too much for the first day of class, but it's a way for me to build authority, to be seen as capable, to build a credible writing teacher ethos with my students. It works well, I must say, and they accept me as the authority completely. But immediately after, I ask them to write down their own mini-histories, their own personal narratives of how they got to *where they are now*, however they define that place. I am often struck by the intimacy of some of the details students share in this impromptu essay, something they probably have never done before, but my goal of creating an open and welcoming environment is almost always set by this reciprocal activity. And because it is reciprocal, this activity also disrupts my authority. By having students write and share these mini-histories in class at the beginning of the semester, they begin to realize that their contributions help create the class, that their participation is what drives the learning in the classroom, and that their narratives are just as important, if not more so, than my own.

Furthermore, as a nonnative, I find that my outsider position affords me great latitude to ask my students questions they wouldn't normally think about or ask themselves, forcing them to regard more critically their closely held beliefs about certain subjects and issues. Indeed, my questions are genuine: I *really* want to know. I once opened a discussion with the question "Why are talk shows so popular in America?" and ended up having an intriguing and energetic discussion on Noam Chomsky and mass media consumption. I find that if we start with topics that students regard as everyday and proceed with intriguing, incisive questions, we often end up analyzing them in their cultural, social, political, and sometimes philosophical contexts.

Moreover, it is essential that my students themselves become responsible for their own ways of meaning-making and acquisition of knowledge, which means creating documents that will fulfill these objectives. So, whenever I require my students to lead class discussion, they also write their own discussion questions and short synthesis essays, which they share with the class. These provide them with opportunities to interrogate one another, refute each other's arguments, and produce clearer, more penetrating insights. More important, I see these as becoming moments for disruption. I once had a student, a Muslim Pakistani, lead a discussion of Naomi Shihab Nye's essay "To Any Would-Be Terrorist." He requested everyone in class to close their eyes and listen to him reading his made-up news report, about American terrorists flying a plane into one of Pakistan's buildings. You can just imagine the discussion we had that day. It ranged from issues of fear and paranoia to global consequences of terror and the future of the United States. It's remarkable how much more open and eager students become, how much braver they get when analyzing difficult issues, and how dramatically their writing improves once they know they can depend on and learn from one another, and not just from the teacher. In short, students both constitute and generate their own learning. This atmosphere of mutual learning helps them realize that they are an active part of an academic community that is continually evolving, questioning, thriving, and very much alive, a community that values their own contributions that make them into that very community.

Writing to name also means disruption in writing. This means learning the rules and knowing when to break them, memorizing the formulae and choosing to ignore them. The key is to expose students to various genres of writing, get them to think about what writing *should* do, how language works, and then provide them with strategies for *how* to accomplish those aims. They may use one or a combination or even none of these strategies, but in the end, students come away more confident and armed with a variety of rhetorical approaches to writing about any topic. I like for my students to become cognizant of the rhetorical situation in each piece of text, probing for content, structures, language, ways of thinking, audience, and types of evidence. I often turn to the genres of fiction, autobiography, and ethnography to show how language moves from one genre to another and how language can be wielded to serve one's rhetorical aims. Short writing assignments are scaffolded and given as stages of invention, all in the service of the major writing assignments.

For example, when students write about their field sites, I have them work on the element of point of view in smaller writing projects that scaffold toward the larger ethnographic project. The first short writing assignment might ask them to describe their field site (e.g., the college cafeteria, the main quad, dormitory lounge, etc.) from their unique perspective, using their own personal voice. Then the second short assignment asks them to describe the same site in an objective, almost clinical, voice. A third assignment asks them to again write about the same place, but this time from the point of view of one of the members or participants from that site. Students often have difficulty writing the second assignment, complaining that they can't be objective enough. Other students have difficulty with the third assignment, saying that writing in another's voice is intrusive to their own research goals.

Inspired by Margery Wolf's *A Thrice-Told Tale*, all three assignments offer critical lessons on the value of ethos and empathy, two elements that I consider constitutive of any writing project (and certainly germane to any ethnographic research). First, taken together, these assignments help students learn the lesson that writing is never objective, that writing to name who you are as a writer informs their written work and shapes the research they perform in the field and the knowledge they share with others. In short, ethos creates logos. Second, students learn that empathy or walking in another person's shoes and working to tell both the writer's and the research subject's stories together make for highly engaging writing. In this sense, students learn that writing is not all that lonely an endeavor, that writing can be a communal art, one that is shared between writer, subject, and reader.

Performing empathy, moving between genres, challenging rules, diffusing authority, teaching with reciprocity, asking genuine, critical questions—these classroom practices constitute what Kerschbaum calls *difference-as-relation*, which "drives communicative efforts because it is part of the interplay between identification and differentiation" (66). In Kerschbaum's view, difference-as-relation is important for teachers to make because it shifts the emphasis away from *learning about others* (which sees identity as fixed) to *learning with others* (which sees difference as relational and emerging in interaction) (74). Such practices embody a translingual perspective, which "recognizes translation and the renegotiation of meaning as operating in all language acts[,] . . . inevitably engaging the labor of recontextualizing (and renewing) language, language practices, users, conventions, and contexts" (Lu and Horner 585–86).

This process of disruption and writing to name appeals to me because of its explicit social reform component, a huge part of why I decided to pursue the field of composition and rhetoric in the first place. It is a critical, public pedagogy that echoes Henry Giroux's *border pedagogy*, in which students engage knowledge as border-crossers, as people moving in and out of borders constructed around coordinates of difference and power. These are not only physical borders, but also cultural borders historically constructed and socially organized within maps of rules and regulations that either limit or enable particular identities, individual capacities, and social forms. Students cross borders of meaning, maps of knowledge, social relations, and values that are increasingly being negotiated and rewritten as the codes and regulations that organize them become destabilized and reshaped. Border pedagogy decenters as it remaps (136).

In Giroux's view, instructors should acquire a great reserve of cultural fluency and sensitivity to students, whether White or of color, native or nonnative, who have widely varying degrees of knowledge and connection to their histories, traditions, and identities. This seems like a tall order to ask of teachers, for it assumes becoming an astute global citizen in the classroom, and, admittedly, we cannot know and teach everything about everyone all the time. But with the continuing enrollment in greater and greater numbers of multilingual, multicultural students, we really have no choice.

My experience may not be all that different from or unique among the experiences of other nonnative teachers. I find comfort and solidarity in that knowledge. Others have said what I'm saying in this essay and it still bears repeating: as teachers and scholars of composition, rhetoric, and communication, it is incumbent on us to continually use language that is historically aware, culturally sensitive, and politically responsible. We must constantly ensure that the language we use is welcoming, inviting, and respectful of one another's differences. The demands of twenty-first-century education compel each of us to practice a potent mix of reading, writing, and enacting. I see writing to name as essential to that mix.

Coda: Passport to the Future

Returning from Manila in the summer of 2015, my first visit since graduating and landing a job, I am anxious as I wait in line again for my turn to be interviewed, fingerprint-scanned, and photographed at the US immigration counter at JFK airport. I have, of course, my passport, newly designating my H1B visa status (see Figure 4.5). And like several times before, I have brought along several documents ready to be presented in case I am asked to do so (I always am)—my birth certificate (now amended), my diplomas, my transcripts, and my I-20s. Now I am also carrying (new documents this past year) my job offer letter, copies

FIGURE 4.5. *The author's US visa, redacted by the author.*

of some recent paychecks, copies of some publications, and my H1B petition submission (all fifty-one pages of it, as advised by my college's lawyers). I look to the line on my right, the shorter line for US citizens and permanent residents, and I think, "Soon, very soon . . ."

Finally, my turn comes. The immigration officer takes my passport, turns to the visa page, scans my fingerprints, takes my photo, hands back my passport, and wishes me good day. It takes no more than two minutes. I present no other document.

I feel the significance of this moment. In a year's time, I will have my green card. Then five years later, I can apply for citizenship, and my brown passport will be given up for a blue one. Maybe all of this will come to pass, maybe not; who knows?

But there, past the immigration counter, with my passport in one hand and the stack of other documents in the other, I find myself again at another boundary, facing another of Bhabha's bridges. I feel "something begin its presencing." Do I acknowledge it? Do I cross the bridge?

I take a deep breath, I look in front of me, and I lift my foot.

Works Cited

Ahmad, Aijaz. *In Theory: Classes, Nations, Literatures.* Verso, 1992.

Bhabha, Homi K. *The Location of Culture.* Routledge, 1994.

Bourdieu, Pierre. *Language and Symbolic Power.* Edited by John B. Thompson, translated by Gino Raymond and Matthew Adamson, Harvard UP, 1991.

Chan, Adrienne S. "Women at the Boundaries." *Forum on Public Policy Online,* no.2, 2010, pp. 1–16. Accessed 10 Feb. 2019.

Dancy, T. Elon II, and M. Christopher Brown II. "The Mentoring and Induction of Educators of Color: Addressing the Impostor Syndrome in Academe." *Journal of School Leadership,* vol. 21, no. 4, 2011, pp. 607–34.

Edbauer, Jenny. "Unframing Models of Public Distribution: From Rhetorical Situation to Rhetorical Ecologies." *Rhetoric Society Quarterly,* vol. 35, no. 4, 2005, pp. 5–24.

Giroux, Henry A. *Border Crossings: Cultural Workers and the Politics of Education.* Routledge, 1992.

Guerra, Juan C. *Language, Culture, Identity and Citizenship in College Classrooms and Communities.* Routledge and National Council of Teachers of English, 2016.

Hayakawa, S. I., and Alan R. Hayakawa. *Language in Thought and Action.* 5th ed., Harcourt, 1990.

Herrmann, Rachel. "Impostor Syndrome Is Definitely a Thing." *The Chronicle of Higher Education,* 2016, www.chronicle.com/article/Impostor-Syndrome-Is/238418. Accessed 23 Mar. 2018.

hooks, bell. *Talking Back: Thinking Feminist, Thinking Black.* South End Press, 1989.

Jarratt, Susan C. "Beside Ourselves: Rhetoric and Representation in Postcolonial Feminist Writing." *Crossing Borderlands: Composition and Postcolonial Studies,* edited by Andrea A. Lunsford and Lahoucine Ouzgane, U of Pittsburgh P, 2004.

Kerschbaum, Stephanie L. *Toward a New Rhetoric of Difference.* National Council of Teachers of English, 2014.

Lu, Min-Zhan, and Bruce Horner. "Translingual Literacy, Language Difference, and Matters of Agency." *College English,* vol. 75, no. 6, 2013, pp. 582–607.

Maulucci, Mária S. Rivera, and Felicia Moore Mensah. "Naming Ourselves and Others." *Journal of Research in Science Teaching,* vol. 52, no. 1, 2015, pp. 1–5. Accessed 20 Sept. 2015.

Minh-ha, Trinh T. *Woman, Native, Other: Writing Postcoloniality and Feminism.* Indiana UP, 2009.

Solórzano, Daniel G., and Tara J. Yosso. "Critical Race Methodology: Counter-Storytelling as an Analytical Framework for Education Research." *Qualitative Inquiry,* vol. 8, no. 1, 2002, pp. 23–44. Accessed 10 Feb. 2019.

Spivak, Gayatri Chakravorty. "Can the Subaltern Speak?" *Marxism and the Interpretation of Culture,* edited by Cary Nelson and Lawrence Grossberg, U of Illinois P, 1988, pp. 271–313.

———. *The Post-Colonial Critic: Interviews, Strategies, Dialogues.* Edited by Sarah Harasym, Routledge, 1990.

Thompson, Jay Daniel. "'I'm not worthy!'—Imposter Syndrome in Academia." *The Research Whisperer*, 2 Feb. 2016, www.theresearchwhisperer.wordpress.com/2016/02/02/imposter-syndrome/. Accessed 23 Mar. 2018.

Williams, Raymond. *Marxism and Literature*. Oxford UP, 1977.

Wolf, Margery. *A Thrice-Told Tale: Feminism, Postmodernism, and Ethnographic Responsibility*. Stanford UP, 1992.

Woolf, Virginia. *The Waves*. Harcourt Brace, 1931.

CHAPTER FIVE

A Right to My Language: Personal and Professional Identity as a "First-Generation" Teacher-Scholar-Rhetorician

LETIZIA GUGLIELMO
Kennesaw State University

If there is nothing else that I have learned from these long years of schooling that began for me with mandatory Head Start, it is this: you are always right there in the mix, no matter how much you have been written out, spanning much wider than the token representation that you have been allowed. The lesson plan, the vibe of my classrooms, the possibilities and invitation that I extend to my students for their writing, the construction of my academic identity, the way I flow with the pen/keypad and paper/screen, all that starts right here with this history. I say all of this to stress that my need for a history in which to place myself was a need that ran very deep. I wasn't going to be able to teach, think, or write without it. Intellectual rootedness in your own histories and a

---

*I use quotation marks around the term "first generation" deliberately here to mark it as unstable and imperfect, and as one that might be replaced by Morris Young's term "first generation American-born" (14) to indicate that while terms such as *first-* and *second-generation* or *Generation 1.5* gesture to citizenship and birthplace, they do not fully capture the varied experiences of immigrants, children of immigrants, and immigrant children who may have varied "immigrant" identities regardless of official immigrant or citizenship status. Placed where it is in the title, the modifier *first-generation* also gestures toward my status as a first-generation college student and academic, signaling that these identities are multiple and overlapping.

scholarly trajectory from which to launch yourself are everything that matter to me.
—CARMEN KYNARD, "Introduction: Runnin with the Rabbits, but Huntin with the Dogs: On the Makings of an Intellectual Autobiography"

Crafting this chapter—similar to my story of literacy and of conscious language development—has been a journey of reflecting and recovering, of questioning and realization, of silencing and coming to voice. I recognize this story as influenced by and developing in the specter of language and literacy policies, political and economic realities, and social and cultural norms that I have both internalized and attempted to reimagine or resist. As literacy scholars and those scholars specifically engaging the genre of literacy narrative have claimed, our own stories of literacy are always changing and evolving (Brandt). I recognize, then, that this version of my story is not only situated in the autobiographical strands I narrate here but also influenced by the current moment of my professional identity and the multiple theoretical lenses through which I choose to tell this story. The previous version of this narrative or the next, in other words, would demonstrate that evolution. This narration is a performance of literacy, of rhetorical awareness, one that may be read as a "literacy success story" equated with social, cultural, and economic power (Alexander 609), but which I hope also prompts awareness of how "literacy" is often code for upholding and reinforcing dominant systems of oppression, as other scholars have demonstrated (Smitherman; Smitherman and Villanueva; Young; Kynard). In reading my own experiences of literacy and language and identity through the multiple lenses of my work as a feminist rhetorician-teacher-scholar, I recognize that I became an English major and later an English professor not *because of* these experiences—literacy and otherwise—but, perhaps more accurately, because of *how* those experiences taught me to *read,* to *interpret,* and to *perform in/ through* moments of literacy, language, access, citizenship, insider-outsider status. These experiences assure me that our discussions of literacy, of writing, and of what has been termed *translanguaging* and *translingual* writing are opportunities to reflect—and to prompt our students to reflect—on the role of rhetoric and ethos in these complex processes. Always recognizing that language use is entangled with power, that determining which languages and literacies and, in turn, which bodies *count,* is an act of discipline and control, I explore the possibilities for interrogating this power within our classrooms as part of our larger discussions of writing, rhetoric, and communication.

I narrate my story in four acts, "storying" as Melanie Yergeau described it during a 2016 Council of Writing Program Administrators (CWPA) conference plenary talk ("Saturday") and has demonstrated elsewhere, because it "holds potentiality . . . to unsettle, digress, and, ultimately, center those who have traditionally been decentered" in stories about their lives (*Authoring Autism* 25–26). And as this collection's introduction makes clear, it is in gathering and listening actively to "little" narratives that we begin to unravel master narratives that both silence and erase lived experience and discipline marginalized "others." Invoking Aja Martinez's "counterstory" and its potential "to expose, analyze, and challenge stock stories of racial privilege and . . . to strengthen traditions of social, political, and cultural survival and resistance" (70), I use this story to complicate dominant narratives about literacy, language policy, and immigrant status and to call on other teacher-scholars to reflect more deliberately on the connection between those narratives and our field's foundations in rhetoric and rhetorical theory.

Act One: A Beginning

I am the child of immigrants. Both my parents are from southern Italy, having immigrated to the United States as teenagers nine years apart in the 1960s and 1970s. Neither had studied English before immigrating. I am the eldest of two children, born in New York and living the first nine years of my life in a multifamily home with extended family members who primarily spoke Italian. I know that I learned to speak Italian and English somewhat simultaneously, yet I cannot identify the precise moment when I named my literacy as primarily English. My approach to literacy has always been cautious and considered and born out of concern, an intersection of *my* speech and identity with the speech and identities that surrounded me. My mother, reading to me when I was a child, for example, was concerned that I would pick up her accent from her narrating of *Goldilocks and the Three Bears*, that I would somehow be marked linguistically as "other." When I learned to write my name, I furiously, obsessively, filled tablet sheets to practice writing the letter *z,* and I chastised my parents for giving me such a difficult name, both first and last names, in their use of all the vowels, and that inevitably and continuously connect me to my Italian heritage and ethnicity. As with my English literacy, I don't know the precise moment when I, like many contributors to this collection, recognized the value of academic achievement and fluency in English, but both were reinforced and rewarded by my parents. Perhaps this knowing was part of the immigrant bargain Steven Alvarez explores in his research with children of immigrants in New York City. Citing the work of Robert Courtney Smith, Alvarez explains, "The immigrant bargain describes an intergenerational class-based expectation that working-class immigrant parents' sacrifices be redeemed and validated in the future through their children's achievements in US schools" (25). "The immigrant bargain," Alvarez continues, "and the promise of the self-actualized American dream understood as upward mobility within a meritocracy both predicate an intense work ethic with promises for future success" (25). The significance of this narrative for many immigrants, immigrant children, and children of immigrants cannot be understated, especially when considered in tandem with Carmen Kynard's claims regarding "the articulation of schooling, literacy, and liberation [as a] forward march toward middle-class redemption" (3–4). My educational attainment within a US education system—particularly in terms of literacy and language acquisition—would not only signal assimilation and acceptable citizenship, but also solidify an "upward mobility" toward middle-class status that performed Americanness both for myself and my parents.

    I am five years old, in kindergarten. My parents and I have just returned from an extended visit in Italy; my memory of the story is that we were there for two or three weeks visiting family and celebrating December holidays. I remember these details because of the photos in the photo album and how my mother has narrated the story when I've tried to reconstruct this part of the memory. In the classroom, my kindergarten teacher asks me a question, and I answer in Italian. She is blond and light-skinned and petite, and she teaches a classroom full of children who speak many languages at home. I think I do this more than once, answer in Italian. I am exhibiting dual language skills; I am bilingual, as are many of my peers, but soon I am ushered off to another classroom, one for students who do not speak English . . . well . . . yet. I quickly catch on and protest. I explain that I *do* know how to speak English, that I *can* answer the questions in English, but the ESL teacher—an Italian American man my memory tells me—insists that the practice will be good for me in this class with the other students who don't speak English . . . well . . . yet. And in some moment during this protest I decide that the experience will be good for me and for them because I can *help* them to speak English as well as I can. I can teach them not to speak anything but English in school. And as I reflect on this memory, whether it is he who insists that I stay to help the other children or I who rationalize my utility in the process of language assimilation, I read and re-read this event in various ways at various points in my story of literacy. I both protest and conform, perform and reject my Italian identity.

Familiarity with a history of immigration, civil rights, and language policies in the United States makes me aware that being born to immigrant parents in New York in the late 1970s placed me in a particularly significant historical moment that was shaped by a loosening of restrictions on immigration by the 1965 Immigration and Nationality Act, a rethinking of language diversity in the classroom through the Bilingual Education Act in 1968, and discussions on language policy in our field that shaped the 1974 "Students' Rights to Their Own Language Resolution" (Smitherman; Bruch and Marback). According to Ofelia Garcia,

> The passage of the Bilingual Education Act was part of an effort to dissipate the growing anger in the nation about injustices and inequities, specifically those surrounding the education

A Right to My Language

of language-minority students. Although the emphasis of the Bilingual Education Act was clearly on teaching English literacy to poor children of "limited English speaking ability," the intent was to provide equal educational opportunity to these children. (134)

Yet later in 1974, reauthorization of the Bilingual Education Act shifted its efforts rhetorically in a significant way, "defin[ing] bilingual education as transitional and remedial" (Garcia 136). "[A]s bilingual education fell into disfavor," Garcia continues, "structured English immersion became the most commonly utilized strategy in the education of emergent bilinguals" (145). Considering my experience within this broader context, my move to an ESL class was, perhaps, grounded in these varied and evolving beliefs of "equal educational opportunity" and "transitional and remedial" support as I developed English language and literacy. To have had access to an ESL classroom just down the hall certainly indicates a need within my elementary school for these pedagogical resources and a commitment on the part of local educators to support students' language development. Yet in attempting to transition out of that classroom as quickly as possible, I read the experience as a sign that I was not to speak Italian in public, especially in school, and that I was to claim a singular literacy if I was to perform appropriate academic achievement. Also undeniable, then, is the significance of this event in determining (or naming) and disciplining my language and literacy for many years to come.

In truth, this experience was made salient against the backdrop of my Italian fluency and literacy, also bound up in language policy and political reality and in the history of Italy's unification in the late nineteenth century. Italy's linguistic history has been described as "chaotic," with collections of languages, variously described as dialects and accents by linguists, that connect speakers to the country's once distinct and very separate kingdoms. "During unification," the story goes,

> the northern Italian powers decided that having a country that speaks about a dozen different languages would pose a bit of a challenge to their efforts, so they picked one and called it "Standard Italian" and made everyone learn it. The one that

they picked was Tuscan, and they probably picked it because it was the language of Dante, the most famous Italian writer. (Nosowitz)

I learn from my mother early on that the Italian I often hear around me at home and at relatives' homes is a dialect, a version of Italian I must understand in order to communicate with family members but one that is inevitably marked and, in many ways, growing archaic. This lesson is reinforced during a trip to Italy in 1988 when I'm talking to other children my age and they giggle at the funny way I speak Italian. It is through Italian, then, that I first learn the rhetorical function and significance of code switching, of language and literacy as performance and power and of an appeal to ethos embedded within the version of Italian I chose to—was able to—speak.

My early experiences in school refined this understanding, demonstrating that English literacy provided a sure path to assimilation and to American prosperity, to legitimacy and to performing appropriate Americanness. I could not have known it at the time, of course, but these teachings would inevitably contribute to language loss as well.

Act Two: A New York Yankee in Andrew Jackson's Court

I am sixteen, and we have just moved from New York to a suburb of Nashville, Tennessee, with the American automobile manufacturer my father works for. My father is a blue-collar auto worker, and facing a plant closing in New York just before I graduate from high school, he and my mother make the difficult decision to move our family to Tennessee. I am now attending a public school in an affluent suburb because it offers the greatest number of Advanced Placement (AP) courses, and it seems like the right choice for my and my sister's education. I am in an English class on the very first day of school, and the teacher is blonde and light-skinned and petite. So are many of the students around me. On that first day of class, there is an icebreaker: we are asked to find a partner, to ask each other questions, and then to introduce our

A Right to My Language

partner to the class with an original poem. My partner is Aubrey. She has dark hair too, and she is the friendliest girl I meet that day. Aubrey was new to the school once, not too long before, and I am smiling and laughing as I construct a poem to introduce Aubrey. I have been asked to use the beginning letters and sound of her name /a-u/ to identify key words for my poem: *awesome, August, draw, sauce*. It's my turn to read my poem to the class, and I repeat Aubrey's name and the /a-u/ sound again and again in each sentence. And with each sentence the class erupts with giggles and laughter. I am a good writer; that's what I learned in my English classes in New York, and maybe I'm funny too. Maybe this place won't be so bad, I think, and I will make friends and I will fit in. And then I realize that they are not laughing at the absurd combination of descriptors I have given my new friend Aubrey; they are laughing *at* me, at my thick New York accent in an English classroom in middle Tennessee, at how funny it sounds when I say *Aubrey* and *awesome* and *August*. As class ends, another student comes over with a smile, and I turn to her eagerly and she says, "Say *Aubrey* again!"

In the weeks and months that follow, I try to make *pen* sound like *pin* because in Tennessee (and in much of the US South), as I very quickly discover, the words have the same pronunciation (see Brown), and I enunciate the /e-r/ in *drawer* so that it doesn't sound like *draw*. Laura Gonzales, in her research exploring multimodality and translingualism among L2 students (defined by the author as "students who speak and write in English as a second language"), explains, "students who have a history of broad linguistic transitions may be especially adept at generating cues across languages and modes based on their extensive experiences code-switching (both linguistically, culturally, and often times transnationally)" (146). Similarly, drawing from the work of Larsen-Freeman and Cameron, Garcia explains that bilinguals engage in "the constant adaptation of their linguistic resources in the service of meaning-making in response to the affordances that emerge in the communicative situation, which is, in turn, affected by learners' adaptability" (146). Here Gonzales and Garcia help me to theorize how and why I was able to quickly adapt my language, to identify the nuances of speech and dialect, to code switch: because I, like many contributors to this collection, instinctively recognized language and literacy as fluid and not fixed, as a process of making rhetorical and discursive choices to adapt to situation and context. But this explanation is complicated by other moments in the crowded halls of that high school, as when someone shouts "Yankee!" as I walk past, and when I'm asked where am I *really* from (meaning some foreign place beyond New York and beyond US borders), and if my family is in the witness protection program because why else would a girl with a name like that who looks like me move to middle Tennessee? These moments of not belonging, of outsider status, may be signaled by my speech, attributed perhaps to language and literacy, but they are made whole when I am asked, "What kind of name *is* that?" and in the way people's eyes narrow and their heads tilt at the sound of my mother's accent. Experiences like these, Morris Young explains, "illustrate the complicated relationship among literacy, race, and citizenship that exists in our culture. The ability to participate in public discourse, to be perceived as fully literate (and without an accent) often becomes a marker of citizenship and legitimacy" (6). "Language," he continues, "or for my purposes, literacy, becomes a guise under which issues of culture and citizenship can be discussed" (55).

Having mastered English literacy, my experience in another part of the country in which I was a citizen, in which I performed "appropriate," assimilated language practices for many years, calls into question our broader connections between literacy, citizenship, and appeals to ethos. Aristotle's introduction to and discussion of ethos in *On Rhetoric* suggest, alternately, that ethos both resides in a rhetor's character and results from the rhetor's words (22, 39, 148–52). Made up of goodwill, good sense, and good character (112), ethos, according to Aristotle and to many first-year writing instructors who theorize this rhetorical appeal with students, is identifiable, visible, and performed—in character and word—for an audience to whom or with whom the rhetor speaks. Equally significant, however, and often less theorized in our classroom discussions of these appeals is the audience's active role in granting or sanctioning that ethos, complicating the appeals of marginalized rhetors within the dominant culture. A significant body of work disrupting classical notions of ethos grows out of feminist rhetorical theory, in which feminist rhetoricians like Krista Ratcliffe remind us, "As scholars too numerous to name have claimed, Aristotle's brilliantly conceived systematic art of rhetoric has greatly influenced Western culture. Yet . . . Aristotle's rhetoric also poses potential pitfalls for women and feminists and, hence, suggests many possible starting points for revisionist theories" (92). Highlighting its embodied quality, Ratcliffe claims, discussions of ethos "traditionally [have] not included a space for women whose sex is visibly marked on their bodies" (93), and here, I would argue, for marginalized rhetors more broadly who embody a marginalized status in the eyes of their audiences.

Gloria Anzaldúa argues "that ethos is a privileged notion that ensures that a particular culture—the dominant one—will continue to flourish" (qtd. in Foss, Foss, and Griffin 122). "The traditional conception of ethos," she continues, "in which audience members assign credibility to rhetors who demonstrate intelligence, moral character, and goodwill, in fact reproduces the cultural expectations of these qualities as credible" (qtd. in Foss, Foss, and Griffin 122). Although "in traditional notions of ethos, rhetors are accorded credibility for being truthful—[by] speaking honestly and in ways that are consistent within the values of the audience," according to Anzaldúa, "marginalized rhetors rarely can speak out of their authentic experiences in the dominant culture" (qtd. in Foss, Foss, and Griffin 122). Recent work on women's ethos by Kathleen J. Ryan, Nancy Myers, and Rebecca Jones, in their edited collection, *Rethinking Ethos: A Feminist Ecological Approach to Rhetoric,* reiterates that "[e]veryday definitions of ethos tend to assume the composing subject is a solitary individual crafting his or her character to firm up reputation and persuasive power" (5), yet we know that women and other marginalized rhetors often are not granted control of their perceived or constructed reputations given social and cultural norms. Moreover, Nedra Reynolds acknowledges "the importance of location, of one's place or perceived location in the world" and argues that "female knowers adapt to their marginalized positions in a male-dominated culture by seeing differently—and learning different things" (325, 330).

My instinct in the space of that high school in Tennessee was to reach for my linguistic resources, aware that language is fluid, and to try to assimilate myself and "my perceived location" to my surroundings. Yet the visible failure of this appeal reiterates that ethos "is a matter of community values" (Ryan, Myers, and Jones 6). Despite having fulfilled some version of the American Dream, that "forward march toward middle-class redemption" (Kynard 3–4), I still fell short of performing appropriate Americanness in the eyes of my evaluators. A "critical literacy approach," according to Alvarez "opens literacy events to reading the gaming of merit, making explicit the structured inequalities of the meritocratic system while also challenging dominant literacies and the status quo" (26). The individual upward mobility myth in the United States, enmeshed with narratives of literacy and "American dreams," often exists at the expense of critical examination of race and class inequalities in the United States. And what is perhaps less fully theorized in our scholarly discussions on literacy, language, and citizenship are rhetorical appeals to ethos: they are not one-sided, not only about performing or establishing an appropriate character, but they are instead about identities established with and sanctioned by the community. Within this specific community, my body was suspect, as is often the case for immigrants, children of immigrants, and minoritized citizens who do not—cannot—adequately perform a White, middle-class ideal in the eyes of their neighbors, peers, and fellow citizens. Young explains, "Intertwined with these literate acts are social contexts that are inextricably tied to the ways we are perceived to be literate. The pleasure and pain of literacy is both public and private, acting in the construction of a sense of self and citizenship" (12). In this way, language and literacy *appear* to be the measures of academic achievement, yet these assessments are part of historic processes of determining and granting citizenship in a country consumed by establishing political, national, and racial boundaries.

In this place, I almost never speak Italian; my younger sister, in fact, never learns the language; and I learn, as Ashanka Kumari describes (this volume), to affect a southern accent when it suits my purposes. If I'm ever asked if I speak Italian, I say, "Not very well" or "Only a few words," because I come to understand—abstractly, at the time—that my language and literacy are intimately connected to my community membership, and in this community

I hesitate to claim an/other language. I recognize that "choosing" English is a rhetorical move intimately connected to my appeals to ethos in this space, a move that signals "dis-identification" with my immigrant and ethnic roots (Alvarez 31–32.).

After graduating from this school in middle Tennessee, I attend Auburn University in Alabama as an undergraduate, but I never make the connection to the first day of English class because I deliberately pronounce that word—Au*burn*—very differently by then. And it is at that university, in the Deep South, that I major in English and minor in Italian to learn how to speak and to write one of my first languages—properly. A true believer in the power of literacy, I am certain that learning to speak and to write Florentine Italian—official Tuscan Italian—will legitimize my Italianness, but when I speak to my family in Italy during a visit at the end of my sophomore year, my sentences feel clumsy and full of too many words, and I find it much easier to speak some hybrid combination of the dialect of my youth and this official language that sounds entirely too formal to be authentic.

Act Three: Imposter Ethos

It is the beginning of my third year in a teaching-intensive faculty position at a university in Georgia. I have a master's degree in English, and I feel like an imposter in an English department and university with many PhDs. Truthfully, I feel like an imposter in this place for many other reasons as well: I am the child of immigrants. I am a first generation college graduate. I am the child of a blue-collar worker. And I am in the academy. I have deferred entrance for one year to more than one doctoral program I have been accepted into because I'm conflicted about giving up a full-time teaching position with health and retirement benefits. And because of this delay, as an instructor, I must go up for a third-year review to show the progress I've made toward possible promotion to assistant professor in three more years and some legitimacy in a tiered system within our department and university. In their influential 1978 article, Pauline Rose Clance and Suzanne Imes identify and articulate the imposter syndrome, a phenomenon among high-achieving women who, "despite their earned degrees, scholastic honors, high achievement on standardized tests, praise and professional recognition from colleagues and respected authorities, . . . do not experience an internal sense of success. They consider themselves to be impostors" (241). The publication date of this piece certainly begs the response that surely "things have gotten better for women" in the last forty years. However, recent admissions by high-profile women such as Tina Fey and Sheryl Sandberg, and continued analysis of imposter syndrome in academic studies (including in other chapters in this collection), suggest that this feeling persists today.

More significant for my purposes here, however, is how feelings of being an imposter compound or contend with the "immigrant bargain" for immigrant children or children of immigrants, and what it means when the "imposter" also has taken a nontraditional path to professorship in a field where contingency in employment status and tiered systems in professorial work are a persistent and significant reality (see Schell; Coalition on the Academic Workforce; "Coalition on Contingent"; Guglielmo and Gaillet; Gaillet and Guglielmo). Clance and Imes's research reveals that foundational experiences underscoring the imposter syndrome begin in childhood, with family members establishing and reinforcing a child's capacity for high achievement, while the child may simultaneously receive contradictory messages from outside the family:

> The child, however, begins to have experiences in which she cannot do any and everything she wants to. She does have difficulty in achieving certain things. Yet she feels obligated to fulfill the expectations of her family, even though she knows she cannot keep up the act forever. Because she is so indiscriminately praised for everything, she begins to distrust her parents' perceptions of her. Moreover, she begins to doubt herself. (243)

Because for me, and for other contributors to this collection, these early experiences involved language and the links between language and community ethos, it seems unsurprising to me now that I pursued an area of study and professional work that allowed me to engage critically and to theorize these connections while also, perhaps unconsciously, allowing me to "master" an area of study that had come to signal assimilation and Americanness for me and for my family. The reality, however, was that this pathway also had the potential to "out" me as illegitimate in ways that moved beyond contingent status and tiered faculty work.

As I received my review letters over the next few months following submission of my review materials, colleagues offered suggestions for organizing my portfolio for future reviews and, more significant, they recommended that I visit Italy and participate in the university's study abroad program. I was stunned. I felt exposed and undermined in some strange way because what I claimed—"chose"—as my teaching and scholarly work was English—writing courses—in which I made no deliberate connection to Italy or to my dual-language beginnings. In this moment of my literacy narrative, as I again reflect on and write about this experience, I understand that it occurs within the specter of all of the other moments when my identity, my legitimacy, was also determined by my language, my name, my geographic "homeland," where I can't escape the ESL classroom and the witness protection program and being asked "where are you *really* from." It feels like further evidence, in other words, that language, identity, and now professional work will be *chosen for me*.

Act Four: Redemption, or Something Like It

It is 2014, ten years after I received those first review letters. I am a tenured associate professor, and I am on my way, for the second time in three years, to study abroad in Italy. Over five weeks, I will live in a Tuscan hill town; teach courses at the intersection of writing, rhetoric, and women's studies; and lead students from Georgia on field trips exploring my "homeland." I will also visit my grandparents in southern Italy, and I will speak Italian. I will speak a combination of Florentine Italian, *dialetto napoletano,* and English. I will clarify for bus drivers where to pick us up and drop us off, because I'm the only faculty member on the trip who speaks Italian "fluently," and I will use this "linguistic capital" (Alvarez 41) to speak to shop owners in Florentine Italian because I know I'll get a better deal. And at dinner with my colleagues one evening, I will ask if anyone wants "cawfee," because in this process of speaking and translating and code switching, all of my hybridity becomes clear. And I realize that the sixteen-year-old New York girl is still in there somewhere.

My teaching and scholarly work in professional writing, rhetoric, and women's studies inform the teaching I do in this study abroad program exploring the rhetorical activities of Renaissance women, women whose voices and experiences were silenced and who made creative appeals to ethos because their "sex [was] visibly marked on their bodies" (Ratcliffe 93). My students and I can create space for these women in our intellectual exchanges because other scholars have recovered their work, and we theorize how members of marginalized groups navigate ethos with visibly hostile audiences in spaces not meant for their bodies. We talk about what this process looks like in the twenty-first century and what it means to create rhetorical spaces in the digital era (see Daniell and Guglielmo). In the States, in a course on rhetoric and US social movements, one of my students asks why we spend so much time discussing ethos, and I explain that appeals to ethos are much more complicated than Aristotle leads us to believe. I begin with Aristotle in this course because of the ways in which his rhetoric can be (and has been) repurposed, disrupted, and remade, and together, my students and I explore how rights activists negotiate a public identity from the margins, allowing them to challenge and to reshape traditional notions of ethos. Drawing from classical rhetoric and from feminist rhetorical scholars, we come to understand how these activists construct "discursive authority [from] the marginal position" (Reynolds 330) and how these appeals are connected to race, citizenship, and legitimacy.

Linking composition and literacy studies as Kynard does, I want my students to recognize that "[t]he intellectual and political intersections between social justice and literacy that we have inherited today have origins in a multiracial, multiethnic Civil Rights Movement that remains the most protracted struggle for equality that the United States has seen" (7–9). What can it look like in our writing and rhetoric courses to disrupt the systems of power that Kynard and other scholars identify, and what might it mean to add the narratives of immigrants and children of immigrants, "ethnic minorities . . . at the bottom of the hierarchy of whiteness" (Kynard 10), and their rhetorical strategies to these disruptions? Morris Young argues,

> While literacy narratives are often employed in the classroom as a way to create pathos and to demonstrate the ethos of writers, to see these writers and their projects as "models" for student writers, they can be even more effective by drawing students into conversations with these narratives. (15)

And as part of these conversations, I would urge us to draw students into more deliberate, nuanced discussions of ethos that acknowledge their roles as audience members, community members, and neighbors who often participate in determining or granting ethos to rhetors in ways that are connected to dominant systems of oppression. Literacy and language use in the United States is as much an issue of performing ethos and citizenship as it is of fluency in reading and writing. An ability to read or write English does not erase the ways in which citizenship is perceived as embodied in the United States and sanctioned—or limited—by community values. "Literacy is always situated, always fulfilling social and cultural purposes" (Kynard 18), and identity—legitimacy—is often determined by accent, name, and imagined geographic "homeland."

In theorizing immigrant experiences as part of more recent scholarship on translanguaging and translingualism, discussions that "giv[e] us a framework for understanding the fluidity of modalities and language" (Gonzales), that cite "translanguaging [as] part of the metadiscursive regimes that students in the twenty-first century must perform, part of a broad linguistic repertoire" (Garcia 147), and that "se[e] difference in language not as a barrier to overcome or as a problem to manage, but as a resource for producing meaning in writing, speaking, reading, and listening" (Horner et al. 303), how might we as teacher-scholars of rhetoric and writing studies, even if we "view the U.S. itself as a transnational space" in our "study of transnational literacy" (Leonard, Vieira, and Young vii, x) and translingual writing in our classroom practice, make room for what it means to be born White and middle class to American-born parents and grandparents rather than to be an immigrant or child of immigrants in that space? What light can the literacy narratives of immigrants and children of immigrants shed on current discussions of translanguaging and translingualism and the ways students' language and literacy practices and performances still operate within and are subject to dominant systems of power outside of (and often within) our classrooms? How might we consider more deliberately the complex rhetorical "negotiation" Paul Kei Matsuda describes that writers and speakers make and that may lead them to reinforce "dominant practices" as deliberate rhetorical choices (480–81), particularly when their questionable ethos or perceived citizenship may be marked on their bodies?

Works Cited

Alexander, Kara Poe. "Successes, Victims, and Prodigies: 'Master' and 'Little' Cultural Narratives in the Literacy Narrative Genre." *College Composition and Communication*, vol. 62, no. 4, 2011, pp. 608–33.

Alvarez, Steven. "Brokering the Immigrant Bargain: Second-Generation Immigrant Youth Negotiating Transnational Orientations to Literacy." *Literacy in Composition Studies*, vol. 3, no. 3, 2015, pp. 25–47.

Aristotle. *On Rhetoric: A Theory of Civic Discourse.* Translated by George A. Kennedy, 2nd ed., Oxford UP, 2007.

Brandt, Deborah. "Accumulating Literacy: Writing and Learning to Write in the Twentieth Century." *College English*, vol. 57, no. 6, 1995, pp. 649–68.

Brown, Vivian R. "Evolution of the Merger of /I/ and /ɛ/ before Nasals in Tennessee." *American Speech*, vol. 66, no. 3, 1991, pp. 303–15.

Bruch, Patrick, and Richard Marback. "Race, Literacy, and the Value of Rights Rhetoric in Composition Studies." *College Composition and Communication*, vol. 53, no. 4, 2002, pp. 651–74.

Clance, Pauline Rose, and Suzanne Imes. "The Imposter Phenomenon in High Achieving Women: Dynamics and Therapeutic Intervention." *Psychotherapy Theory, Research and Practice*, vol. 15, no. 3, 1978, pp. 241–47.

"Coalition on Contingent Academic Labor (COCAL)." *New Faculty Majority*, http://www.newfacultymajority.info/cocal/#.

Coalition on the Academic Workforce (CAW). "A Portrait of Part-Time Faculty Members: A Summary of Findings on Part-Time Faculty

Respondents to the Coalition on the Academic Workforce Survey of Contingent Faculty Members and Instructors." 2012, http://www.academicworkforce.org/survey.html.

Daniell, Beth, and Letizia Guglielmo. "Changing Audience, Changing Ethos." *Rethinking Ethos: A Feminist Ecological Approach to Rhetoric,* edited by Kathleen J. Ryan, Nancy Myers, and Rebecca Jones, Southern Illinois UP, 2016, pp. 89–109.

Foss, Karen A., Sonja K. Foss, and Cindy L. Griffin. *Feminist Rhetorical Theories.* SAGE, 1999.

Gaillet, Lynée Lewis, and Letizia Guglielmo. *Scholarly Publication in a Changing Academic Landscape: Models for Success.* Palgrave Macmillan, 2014.

Garcia, Ofelia. "Educating New York's Bilingual Children: Constructing a Future from the Past." *International Journal of Bilingual Education and Bilingualism,* vol. 14, no. 2, pp. 133–53.

Gonzales, Laura. "Multimodality, Translingualism, and Rhetorical Genre Studies." *Composition Forum,* vol. 31, 2015, http://compositionforum.com/issue/31/multimodality.php.

Guglielmo, Letizia, and Lynée Lewis Gaillet. "Preface: On Being Contingent: Advocating Mentoring and Collaboration." *Contingent Faculty Publishing in Community: Case Studies for Successful Collaborations,* edited by Letizia Guglielmo and Lynée Lewis Gaillet, Palgrave Macmillan, 2015, pp. vii–xiii.

Horner, Bruce, Min-Zhan Lu, Jacqueline Jones Royster, and John Trimbur. "Opinion: Language Difference in Writing: Toward a Translingual Approach." *College English,* vol. 73, no. 3, 2011, pp. 303–21.

Kynard, Carmen. "Introduction: Runnin with the Rabbits, but Huntin with the Dogs: On the Makings of an Intellectual Autobiography." *Vernacular Insurrections: Race, Black Protest, and the New Century in Composition-Literacies Studies.* State U of New York P, 2013, pp. 1–19.

Leonard, Rebecca Lorimer, Kate Vieira, and Morris Young. "Special Editors' Introduction to Issue 3.3." *Literacy in Composition Studies,* vol. 3, no. 3, 2015, pp. vi–xii.

Martinez, Aja Y. "A Plea for Critical Race Theory Counterstory: Stock Story versus Counterstory Dialogues Concerning Alejandra's 'Fit' in the Academy." *Composition Studies,* vol. 42, no. 2, 2014, pp.

33–55. Reprinted in *Performing Antiracist Pedagogy in Rhetoric, Writing, and Communication,* edited by Frankie Condon and Vershawn Ashanti Young, Across the Disciplines Books, WAC Clearinghouse and UP of Colorado, 2016, pp. 65–85, https://wac.colostate.edu/books/atd/antiracist/.

Matsuda, Paul Kei. "The Lure of Translingual Writing." *PMLA,* vol. 129, no. 3, 2014, pp. 478–83.

Nosowitz, Dan. "How Capicola Became Gabagool: The Italian New Jersey Accent, Explained: A Linguistic Exploration." *Atlas Obscura,* 5 Nov. 2015, https://www.atlasobscura.com/articles/how-capicola-became-gabagool-the-italian-new-jersey-accent-explained?utm_source=facebook.com&utm_medium=mentalfloss.

Ratcliffe, Krista. "Bathsheba's Dilemma: Defining, Discovering, and Defending Anglo-American Feminist Theories of Rhetoric(s)." *Anglo-American Feminist Challenges to the Rhetorical Traditions: Virginia Woolf, Mary Daly, Adrienne Rich,* Southern Illinois UP, 1996, pp. 1–31. Rpt. in *Walking and Talking Feminist Rhetorics: Landmark Essays and Controversies,* edited by Lindal Buchanan and Kathleen J. Ryan, Parlor Press, 2010, pp. 80–107.

Reynolds, Nedra. "*Ethos* as Location: New Sites for Understanding Discursive Authority." *Rhetoric Review,* vol. 11, no. 2, 1993, pp. 325–38.

Ryan, Kathleen J., Nancy Myers, and Rebecca Jones, editors. *Rethinking Ethos: A Feminist Ecological Approach to Rhetoric.* Southern Illinois UP, 2016.

Schell, Eileen E. *Gypsy Academics and Mother-Teachers: Gender, Contingent Labor, and Writing Instruction.* Boynton/Cook Heinemann, 1998.

Smitherman, Geneva. "The Historical Struggle for Language Rights in CCCC." *Language Diversity in the Classroom: From Intention to Practice,* edited by Geneva Smitherman and Victor Villanueva, Southern Illinois UP and Conference on College Composition and Communication, 2003, pp. 7–39.

Smitherman, Geneva, and Victor Villanueva, editors. *Language Diversity in the Classroom: From Intention to Practice.* Southern Illinois UP and Conference on College Composition and Communication, 2003.

Yergeau, Melanie. *Authoring Autism: On Rhetoric and Neurological Queerness.* Duke UP, 2017.

———. "Saturday Plenary Address: Creating a Culture of Access in Writing Program Administration." *WPA: Writing Program Administration,* vol. 40, no. 1, 2016, pp. 155–65.

Young, Morris. *Minor Re/Visions: Asian American Literacy Narratives as a Rhetoric of Citizenship.* Southern Illinois UP and Conference on College Composition and Communication, 2004.

CHAPTER SIX

Choosing English: Crafting a Professional Identity as a College Professor

NATALIA KOVALYOVA
The University of Texas at Austin

It is fitting for writing on professional identity to start by revealing the work's own academic origins. This essay began as a hushed conversation with a close friend about frustrations of transitioning from graduate school to a faculty job. A year later it became a panel talk at a national conference and a paper on linguistic insecurity at work. Once in the hands of a journal editor, it morphed into a forum contribution (never published) that would highlight lived experiences through policy change. Further revisions turned it into this current chapter in an edited volume. As the project transformed, so did I—moving through genres, venues, frames, and counterarguments. My inner rhetorician, whose rebellion propelled the paper into existence, acquired new sensitivities, devised new strategies, and renewed a sense of confidence in navigating a diverse, multilingual terrain. Although I have not discovered a magic switch to turn an aspiring international student into a popular professor, I have learned to recognize and resist the moments when one's linguistic, social, cultural, and other assets are degraded into one's liabilities. The road I have traveled, with all its proverbial bumps and detours, is sketched in this essay. I hope that those who follow a similar career path with similar assets find the essay reassuring. For the rest of us, it is intended to highlight the fact that norms around language often (if not always) reaffirm deeply entrenched stereotypes and biases, and that for the purpose of unearthing their impact, telling a nonconforming counterystory might be the best methodology to date.

An Incident on a Language Terrain

At the start of my second semester as a faculty member at a small public university, I received an email request to read a policy chapter (attached to the message) and to fill out a form, also attached. The policy chapter titled "Program of Assistance for Non-Primary English-Speaking Teaching Personnel" referred to the state's education code that mandated public institutions of higher education to establish such programs for nonnative speakers among their employees. I found the request a bit troubling. No one had questioned my language skills or asked for a language proficiency certification at any point in the hiring process. The search committee was able to evaluate my ability to teach without a separate language test. I myself never expressed a wish to be assisted with the English language. The course evaluations were not yet in, so I didn't suspect the all-faculty mailout of the policy chapter to be damage control in the aftermath of massive student complaints. The more I read, though, the more unsettling the document became as it outlined the stages of assessment (a self-report, then a language test), stating in paragraph 2.03 that "as a result of the assessment of language competence, individuals may be required to participate in a program of language assistance as a condition of employment in any teaching capacity." Paragraph 3.04 announced that the cost of participation in the said program "will be paid by the faculty member required to participate." But the culmination of the missive waited inside the form that I was to fill out. It wanted my appropriate pick between two options:

> Option 1
> I _____ [insert the name] _____ attest that English is my primary language and that I do not have any difficulty communicating effectively in English in meeting my teaching obligations.

Option 2
I _____ [insert the name] ___ attest that English is not my primary language. My primary language is _____ [insert the name].

Signed_____ [name & date]

The options were stacked so heavily that I laughed. What should one select if English is their "primary" language but they struggle to understand a variety of local accents that the students proudly demonstrate or to make sense out of their Twitter-inspired spelling and grammar? Do soporific lectures delivered in flawless English count for "communicating effectively"? What about handwritten comments on students' papers decipherable only by a team of trained cryptologists? All of those communicative peculiarities-cum-barriers did not seem to have alarmed the campus office responsible for policy compliance since the primacy of English was somehow deemed to ensure an acceptable—in fact, conflict-free—performance "meeting . . . teaching obligations." A bold merger of language primacy with teaching effectiveness instituted by the coordinate conjunction *and* in Option 1 was hard to overlook and even harder to let go. The absence of a parallel coordinate clause in Option 2 foregrounded the underlying assumptions about the command of English and effective instruction. The legal modality of the key term—not a *native* language, or a *mother tongue*, or a *first* language, but a *primary* language—eliminated a chance to celebrate *nonprimary* ones as a legitimate means of instruction. Finding no definitional cue to anchor my interpretations, I concluded that *primary* could safely mean a language used most of the time (that is, *primarily*) and, since I speak nothing but English eleven months in any given year and write exclusively in English, I selected Option 1 and dropped the form with the provost's secretary.

A few day later I overheard a bitter comment about the language certification request and it resonated with me as well, for I had heard that dog-whistle just as clearly: nonnative English-speaking professors were implicated as struggling in classrooms and other places where "teaching obligations" might take them. Yet, having discovered a loop in the policy wording, I gamed the system, so to speak, and wanted to believe that I had outsmarted whoever had planned to dislodge me as a non-NEST (an acronym coined by Peter Medgyes to refer to nonnative English-speaking teachers). My perception of sudden outing was unmistakable, though.

As a young professor building a career at an American university and a first-generation transplant onto American soil, I diligently worked on making my presentations engaging, my lectures meaningful and memorable, and my writing better than the "horrible ESL academese" that had once disturbed an ad-hoc conference reviewer. I focused on learning activities and timely feedback to students, on the quality of my ideas and clarity of my writing. Of course, I heard about the imposter syndrome, reportedly rampant in academia and affecting anyone from an undergraduate student to a professor but most disproportionately beleaguering women, persons of color, and first-generation students (see Mayshle, this volume). Aware of a self-fulfilling prophecy of a perceived stereotype threat, I put up all the guards I could muster in order not to slide into making excuses for being where I am and "explain[ing] myself to the dominant culture" (Mayshle, this volume). After all, I was among fellow academics, whose training and professionalism, I wanted to believe, should save me from judgment based on ethnic origin, nationality, race, class, gender, physical abilities, and appearance.

Having embraced the idea that identity is always in the making and that it refuses being pinned down by a definitive label of "who I really am," I stayed busy juggling daily tasks and didn't pay much attention to the forces that had been shaping my workplace and that influenced how the "instructional personnel" were imagined on campus. Now I stood in their direct line of fire and needed a survival toolkit for my immediate environment. Two questions felt most urgent: (1) What changes has the policy engendered? and (2) How should I continue personally and professionally under the new circumstances? To proceed, I selected a case study route, keeping a sample of n=1 participants in order to chart the "processes and practices that constructed me" (Goodall 186). I could have begun contextualizing and historicizing the language policy in a university certified as a Hispanic-serving institution. Alternatively, I could have interviewed my colleagues, all of whom received the form, in order to assess changes in the organizational climate created by the policy in question. My decision to adopt a reflective route was motivated by the policy's underlying assumptions about language. I used to treat language as an asset (after all, I'm fluent in three languages and have a working knowledge of an additional two); now anything aside from English was presented as a potential liability. I used to offer personal stories as a way of enriching discussions; now my prior experience was cast to compromise my status; in fact, my performance in the line of professional teaching obligations was possibly inviting a corrective intervention.

Pierre Bourdieu's ideas about different forms of capital and the rules of their conversion helped me locate a conceptual peg for approaching the policy and its consequences ("Forms of Capital"). In what follows, I demonstrate how the language policy has accomplished social gerrymandering among faculty by rhetorically blocking the conversion of individual linguistic resources into symbolic or economic capital. Moreover, I argue that the managerial discourse that generated it strove to interpellate a particular type of worker—disciplined, self-regulating, thoroughly "knowable," and fundamentally insecure. Yet the policy's success was not paramount to the institution. My refusal to validate the implications about language proficiency and teaching abilities cast in sharper relief the arbitrariness of such binaries as native/nonnative and primary/nonprimary and questioned widely spread practices of "norming" and "standardization" of languages and language users. Secretly, though, I hoped that by enlisting myself in the group of "primary" English speakers, I managed to act in a way that rendered impotent the "system of power" (Guglielmo, this volume) with its reliance on the continuity of the "old" dominant group and the continuity of its colonial control over the Other (Cervantes-Rodriguez and Lutz; Flores and Murillo). I wanted to believe that the order imposed on me and my fellow co-workers would crumble because it attempted to pinpoint something that is fluid and constantly evolving, namely, our linguistic and professional identities.

The Letter and the Spirit of Institutional Regulations

As I observed earlier, the underlying logic of the language certification form equated the primacy of English with effective communication in the line of teaching duties, hence the wording in Option 1: "English is my primary language and . . . I do not have any difficulty communicating effectively in English in meeting my teaching obligations." Starting with the equivalence of the two terms—*primacy* and *effectiveness*,—policy unfolded further through the stages of identifying "problem faculty." A self-report was to be followed by a language test and an optional demonstration lecture "to validate English language competence," as stipulated in paragraph 2.01. For those whose assessment yielded negative results, the program of assistance would launch. Failure to demonstrate a satisfactory performance upon its completion would result in termination—all done in the spirit of upholding the status of English as the language of instruction in public schools across the state.

The specifics of the implementation plan, with its emphasis on language performance rather than on the quality of teaching, suggested that the policy long predates my campus and that its roots go back to the English Only movement, with its fear of balkanization. The choice of "intervention" measures also spoke of dated pedagogical practices. The policy chapter recommended a "series of lectures" as a means of "dealing with communication skills, basic techniques for effective teaching and cross-cultural differences in the classroom." Section 3.02 further detailed the envisioned "training" in proper classroom communication: "Individual workshops in which teaching personnel will have the opportunity for one-on-one attention to practice lectures, pronunciation and/or any other appropriate areas of communication and teaching." Notably absent were the mentions of other genres, formats, and situations in which instructors communicate and through which they can be evaluated, such as feedback on student work, consultations during office hours, etc. Criteria for passing as a "competent" speaker also remained unspecified, further obscuring the picture of what besides the nonprimary speakers the policy was countering.

That pronunciation was singled out as a major problem area was a telling sign as well, hinting at deeply seated fears of the accentuated speech of those who speak English as a second, third, or fourth language, fears intensified when nonprimary speakers assume a position of authority in their capacity as college professors. A prolonged struggle over the language of instruction engages views on schools as places where society is being reproduced, that is, as one of the ideological apparatuses that regulate social order (McLaren; Giroux). The idea of requiring a single language as a way of homogenizing the population within the national borders and of holding the "nation" together is not exclusively American (Bryce). Here, however, public conversation about the language of instruction evolves around the rights of children and the equality of access to education resources since in the past some public schools "interpreted their Americanization mission with jingoistic singlemindedness little short of brutality" (Hechinger C4). The debate of what and how to teach in schools goes hand in hand with the question of who stands as a figure of authority in charge of younger generations "in training." In schools—the institutions with an ideological mission—the teaching personnel have to embody it and, preferably, "to speak it" as well. Consequently, nonprimary English is perceived as a marker of a "foreign" body and an indicator of a potential cultural "breach" in schools' social contract to turn out future citizens. This logic evidently guided the language policymakers at my school who recommended mini-lectures on "cross-cultural differences" as part of the program of assistance to nonprimary speakers.

The myth of native speakers of English as the predominant group that got codified in the language policy in question still persists in the national psyche despite numerous studies and linguistic maps of the United States that picture a different reality on the ground. For instance, the 2011 US census reported 20.8 percent of the American population speaking a language other than English at home, thus contributing to an amazing linguistic diversity of 303 different languages spoken within the national borders. A long history of population migration has produced the current linguistic makeup of the United States in which nonprimary speakers of English are often American citizens—born, raised, and schooled here. Some of those nonprimary English speakers select teaching as their vocation of choice and, if they happen to teach in a state in which English has been legislated into the status of official language (or where it is the mandated language of instruction in the institutions of public education), they are bound to trigger the application of language assistance programs they do not need.

Curiously enough, despite the non-NESTs' increasing presence on campuses, they do not enjoy much academic attention. Studies of multilingualism in the classroom tend to discuss literacy backgrounds and skills of minority students classified as such because of their "racial and ethnic (nonwhite) background." Sometimes, a scope of linguistic diversity expands to include "a nonmainstream variety of English" spoken at home by White students (Lovejoy, Fox, and Wills 261). Considerably less recognized is the linguistic diversity among faculty (Pavlenko; Sachs). Still less discussed are their rights to their own language.

In this context, the language policy on my campus forges a position of superiority for primary English speakers and compromises a chance to achieve such a position for differently languaged instructors. Despite its wording suggestive of a mobility ladder (aka the program of assistance) away from the ranks of presumably ineffective instructors with low proficiency in the English language, the "primacy" classifier masks the impossibility of success once the labels are placed, for no provision, corrective, or intervention is capable of altering the order in which languages have been acquired. To emphasize: because the policy's decisive point rests with language primacy and because the order of language acquisition is not amenable to change, the policy engages in a discriminatory divide among the teaching personnel and turns nonprimacy into a source of permanent vulnerability and insecurity. A policy stipulation that the employment of non-NESTs with a "problematic" command of English is to be conditional upon their successful completion of the program and, presumably, upon their believable mimicry of primary speakers reveals the inferior standing of non-NESTs in the eyes of policymakers.

Transactions and Conversions: Bourdieu to the Rescue

A mechanism of exclusion triggered by the language policy and the route of possible countermeasures can be usefully clarified with the help of Pierre Bourdieu's notion of different forms of capital. Bourdieu ("Forms of Capital") posited that in addition to *economic capital* (money, stocks, property, and other forms of material wealth), individuals possess *cultural capital* (knowledge, skills, qualifications, degrees, and cultural practices, norms, and attitudes), *symbolic capital* (accumulated prestige and honor), *social capital* (relationships and connections to other members of the group), and *linguistic capital* (an overall practical competence in language use). In this view, each additional language one speaks makes that person more "resourceful" and more valuable thanks to a range of experiences, knowledge, and practices they have accumulated, have access to, or can leverage. In a workplace, a potential employee fluent in several languages promises to bring skills, knowledge, and contacts not obtainable otherwise and, on these grounds, might negotiate a higher salary. Quite practically, then, language is a cultural asset and a negotiation item in one's personal portfolio. The possibility of a future conversion of linguistic capital into prestige (*symbolic capital*) or higher earnings (*economic capital*) or a better life stimulates a lot of learners to invest years in mastering foreign languages.

However, different fields of human activity establish specific rules of conversion to regulate exchange so that, for example, more education (*cultural* capital) can be traded for a better-paying job (*economic* capital) and/or a higher social status (*symbolic* capital), but what specific education is convertible for what gains depends on a particular field. For instance, an advanced academic degree would hardly translate into a higher social standing in a field that values practical wisdom and manual skills.

According to Bourdieu (*Language*), the language policy under discussion here establishes the rules that block "free trading" of the nonprimary linguistic capital for symbolic or economic gain. Furthermore, because of the conflation between effective instructional communication and a native-like command of English (see again Option 1 in the language certification request), the policy also relegates other forms of cultural capital that non-NESTs might have accumulated. Their investments in education, their years of training to acquire advanced degrees, and their years of classroom experience devalue in comparison to similar investments made by primary English speakers. Eventually, the rich individual "possessions" of multilingual speakers risk becoming dead capital, put out of circulation while a native variety of English turns into the only legitimate linguistic "currency" accepted within the walls of an educational institution.

Insufficient cultural capital referenced as a basis for exclusion is not an uncommon academic scenario and is encountered in many instances—from the "overlooked" key works on the topic to the "wrong" journals to publish in that undermine and, in unhappy instances, derail professors' careers; from the focus on the "product" rather than the "process" of writing to the "strange" formatting that marks a writer socialized in a different field of knowledge (say, electrical engineering instead of composition studies). With serious implications entailed by exclusions from various academic circles, compliance with the local conventions becomes an exercise in self-discipline. Primary English speakers who experience communication "difficulties" in meeting their teaching obligations have to put in additional effort to reason away cognitive dissonance, such as convincing themselves that those "difficulties" are inevitable, perhaps as a function of the subject matter itself. Non-NESTs complying with the policy have to fend off the onset of linguistic insecurity and a state of "perpetual liminality" (Callahan 354)—that is, of constant negotiation of their "outsider" status among cultural and professional communities to which they belong.

Liminal spaces are known to be rife with tension and fear; conversely, they provoke creativity and imagination (if only for survival purposes), and they allow "opportunities to explore different means of communication" and to "migrate" between practices and communities (Palacio, this volume). I have traveled that route as well, albeit not too far, and looked for ways to "convert" myself into a more marketable—and employable—individual, combining my resources and devising my strategies. "If my accent betrays me most of the time," I reasoned, "I should invest in other forms of capital to make it in academe." It didn't take me long to adopt writing as my job-securing strategy. "Professors as writers," I reminded myself, rolling out of bed and reaching for the keyboard. "Writing is what you have been hired to do" was my excuse for a delay in grading. It was almost funny to think that the program of language assistance selected lecturing as the genre to master when so much in the professor's life depends on writing (in understandable English, no less) and publishing. Writing did provide a more secure haven. There, I could navigate the power lines more carefully and at my own pace. Yet I could not pretend to have discovered a politics-free manner of writing. To be a more sensitive rhetorician, I constantly have to trace major contextual forces to identify the decision makers likely to weigh in on my conversion to a tenured professor. But aside from the tenure committee, there are also my students, who watch me living the life of a non-native-English-speaking professor and who come to my class with their own histories of resisting school when (to channel Mark Twain here) it gets in the way of their education. Whose norms are used to evaluate my students' learning and my teaching, who is called upon as a disinterested arbitrator in case of a dispute, and who becomes our go-to authority are always open-ended questions with no correct answers.

The state education code that has engendered language policies on individual campuses unequivocally indicates its goal as "ensur[ing] that courses offered for credit at the institution are taught in the English language and that all faculty members are proficient in the use of the English language." Thus, its foundational assumption is that exposure to instruction in nonprimary English inflicts some harm on students and that, in the best interests of the students, they should be protected from such exposure. Just who those students are is hard to pinpoint. My campus is quite diverse and proudly showcases much bounty in looks—dreadlocks, full veil, ponytails, baseball caps, military and police uniforms—as well as in ethnic composition: 41 percent Hispanic, 35 percent African American, 17 percent Caucasian, and 3 percent Asian, with the remaining 4 percent identified as international students or other (Office of Strategic Analysis). Such demographics embrace diverse identities, rich family histories, idiosyncratic home languages, less than straightforward paths to college, and varied educational experiences (Matsuda). Indeed, a recurring motive in my students' literacy essays is being misclassified as "ESL."

Coming from different backgrounds, linguistic and otherwise, students work out their own unique ways of "doing college," often starting from a personal experience of being "an outsider in academia" (Shaughnessy qtd. in Lu and Horner 213). Some ask questions and engage in discussions but remain indifferent to written work; others sit quietly through the class yet submit assignments that any teacher would dream of receiving; some already "know" that their future jobs are not going to require writing; still others blossom as incredible storytellers. There are those who worry about coming across as disrespectful while their classmates challenge my every word. Our differences do not always align or compare: I never had to serve as a language broker for my family, and, as an academic brat, I tended to see my professors as "my kind of people." Still, we can learn from one another how to make the most out of college in order to succeed in life upon graduation (for them) and to keep a job past their graduation (for me). A useful starting point in our joint project of "figuring out" college is our common experience of navigating the language norms and linguistic stereotypes so that we can construct a nuanced understanding of where the "standards" come from, how they condition our personal and collective lives, under what pressure they would give in to the restrictions of those standards, and how we can read the social and political context to align our resources and linguistic choices for better results. Equipped with that knowledge, we, now smarter rhetoricians, can proceed to craft our narratives and our lives.

Joining Forces with Students

Bourdieu's market-grounded metaphors described earlier help identify "capitals" and the patterns of their conversion in the academic world (*Language*). It is important to remember, however, that metaphors hide as well as reveal, and that alternative framing, subject positions, coalitions, and lines of action are possible. Once the "natural" superiority of primary language gets demystified and the "norm" democratized, one soon discovers new potential partners and can forge new alliances based on more democratic terms. Such regrouping will most certainly require us to reconsider (and, ultimately, discard) the apprentice model in which students appear as novices and professors as discourse masters. A new configuration of our relationship will call on both parties to negotiate "the structures of schooling," to probe their solidity (Gilyard 286), and to find out just how malleable the norms and contingent the language might be.

An orientation toward language use that recognizes its contingency, arbitrariness, and ideological loading has been developing within a translingual approach to language and language users. Translingualism shares a number of core propositions with other theoretical approaches that highlight the role of discourse in power formations, most importantly with critical pedagogy and Foucauldian discourse studies (Guerra; Horner, Lu, Jones Royster, and Trimbur). It also emphasizes the uniqueness of differences among language users and warns against the "flattening" of those differences (Gilyard 286). LuMing Mao coined a wonderful term to capture the relationship between different rhetorics as they "mingle, negotiate, and further contend with other discourses"; he calls this paradigm "interdependence-in-difference" (qtd. in Ray 95). Accordingly, in a multilingual classroom, the relationship between professors and students hinges on such interdependence since both parties are negotiating, contending, and compromising. The necessary presence (emphasis on *necessary*) of other people and their views on "who you are" is one of the best kept secrets of contemporary society regarding identity. Contrary to folk beliefs, there is no essential, "true" self that is accessible only to its owner, largely in introspection, and that should be defended at all costs from the infringements of others. In fact, to fully know oneself, one needs other people's perspectives on how one comes across—hence "interdependence." Identity is never one's own production, it is never complete, and, from the stories we have heard so far in this collection, it is the opposite of blending in and seeking security by being indistinguishable (Mayshle, this volume).

A translingual lens on language practices in the classroom, on campus, and in society inevitably directs us to discern ideas, discourses, frames, and stylistic devices that are assembled in specific contexts in order to normalize a certain state of affairs and certain language practices while marking other language practices and language users as deviant (or, in the parlance of the policy document I'm discussing here, lacking proficiency). As Keith Gilyard observed, translingualists are particularly attuned to the repressive deployment of language standards in select cases and their restrictive nature across the board (284). They are particularly well equipped to identify the administrative decisions informed by a language ideology that sorts people into those who meet and those who fall short of a fantastic concoction called "standard English."

To work out a viable strategy for handling the forces that advance this ideology, we might start cultivating rhetorical sensitivities toward language as situational, subjective, and largely political, rather than fixed and overdetermined by a strict and stable system of rules. Such sensitivities should be aligned with the idea that norms are social constructs and, therefore, subject to change by evolutionary as well as revolutionary means. Astute rhetoricians always attend to a situation by evaluating in it the available means of persuasion and their projected effectiveness. In other words, they focus on what language can accomplish and what it does for us and to us, which brings me to my last point—the process of identity formation, linguistic as well as professional.

The language policy incident I described earlier initially shook me out of my comfort zone of a (relatively) successful academic and alerted me to the unfinished nature of identity work. It raised many questions that lay dormant or were retired to the backstage of my daily life, not because of their insignificance but because I suspected Herculean efforts were needed to sort them out. I dodged the challenge of rebranding myself (or, failing that, of constructing a protective belt around my multilingual self) not once but twice. I completed my PhD in the same state where I found my first faculty position, and, as an incoming international student back then, I had to take a speaking test to demonstrate proficiency in English before I could be placed as a teaching assistant. The language policy was in place, promising to assist potential "problem cases" among the university's teaching personnel, graduate TAs included. With a master's degree from an American university in hand, I requested exemption. My argument that an advanced degree and 4.0 GPA constituted sufficient evidence of my language proficiency carried little weight. No degree could erase my status as a nonnative English speaker. Scoring 300 out of 300 points available on the test, I made a mental remark of "I told you so" and moved on. Writing a dissertation felt more pressing than making sense of an intricate lattice of perceptions, constructs, and roles spun around me. Four years later and 200 miles to the north of my home campus, that unprocessed reality caught up with me.

Identity work is never easy, no matter how effortlessly the statement "I know who I am" rolls off myriad tongues, mine included, and, unfortunately, that work cannot be outsourced. Moreover, the answer to the question of who I am requires other people to calibrate it. For a college professor, those people make quite a crowd, including colleagues, family, friends, students (and their parents), and, yes, the administration. Their views of me are indispensable to what I make of myself, although nobody involved is privileged to an exclusive and final version of "me." In my current endeavor to confidently position myself as a college professor, I claim English as a constitutive part of myself because I have learned something important about the world and about "languaging" against the sterility of standards and the attributed supremacy of the primary order of acquisition. I have learned that having a language comes alive in doing language, and the latter, as Toni Morrison teaches us, is a measure of our life.

Works Cited

Aquino-Sterling, Cristian R., and Fernando Rodríguez-Valls. "Developing Teaching-Specific Spanish Competencies in Bilingual Teacher Education: Toward a Culturally, Linguistically, and Professionally Relevant Approach." *Multicultural Perspectives*, vol. 18, no. 2, 2016, pp. 73–81. EBSCO*host*, doi:10.1080/15210960.2016.1152894.

Bourdieu, Pierre. "The Forms of Capital." *Handbook of Theory and Research for the Sociology of Education*, edited by John Richardson, Greenwood, 1986, pp. 241–58.

———. *Language and Symbolic Power*. Harvard UP, 1991.

Bryce, Benjamin. "Linguistic Ideology and State Power: German and English Education in Ontario, 1880-1912." *Canadian Historical Review*, vol. 94, no. 2, 2013, pp. 207–33. EBSCO*host*, doi:10.3138/chr.1463.

Callahan, Sara B. Dykins. "Academic Outings." *Symbolic Interaction*, vol. 31, no. 4, 2008, 351–75.

Cervantes-Rodriguez, Ana Margarita, and Amy Lutz. "Coloniality of Power, Immigration, and the English-Spanish Asymmetry in the United States." *Nepantla: Views from South*, vol. 4, no. 3, 2003, pp. 523–60. EBSCO*host*, ezproxy.lib.utexas.edu/login?url=http://search.ebscohost.com/login.aspx?direct=true&db=a9h&AN=11868551&site=ehost-live.

Flores, Susana Y., and Enrique G. Murillo, Jr. "Power, Language, and Ideology: Historical and Contemporary Notes on the Dismantling of Bilingual Education." *Urban Review*, vol. 33, no. 3, 2001, pp. 183–206. EBSCO*host*, ezproxy.lib.utexas.edu/login?url=http://search.ebscohost.com/login.aspx?direct=true&db=a9h&AN=11308923&site=ehost-live.

Gilyard, Keith. "The Rhetoric of Translingualism." *College English*, vol. 78, no. 3, 2016, pp. 284–89.

Giroux, Henry A. *Theory and Resistance in Education: A Pedagogy for the Opposition*. Bergin & Garvey, 1983.

Goodall, Harold Lloyd, Jr. "Commentary: Narrative Ethnography as Applied Communication Research." *Journal of Applied Communication Research*, vol. 32, no. 3, 2004, pp. 185–94.

Guerra, Juan C. "Cultivating a Rhetorical Sensibility in the Translingual Writing Classroom." *College English*, vol. 78, no. 3, 2016, pp. 228–33.

Hechinger, Fred M. "About Education; U.S. Ruling Fuels Controversy over Bilingual Teaching." *The New York Times*, 20 Jan. 1981, p. C4.

Horner, Bruce, Min-Zhan Lu, Jacqueline Jones Royster, and John Trimbur. "Language Difference in Writing: Toward a Translingual Approach." *College English*, vol. 73, no. 3, pp. 303–21.

Lovejoy, Kim Brian, Steve Fox, and Katherine V. Wills. "From Language Experience to Classroom Practice: Affirming Linguistic Diversity in Writing Pedagogy." *Pedagogy: Critical Approaches to Teaching*

Literature, Language, Composition, and Culture, vol. 9, no. 2, 2009, pp. 261–87.

Lu, Min-Zhan, and Bruce Horner. "Introduction: Translingual Work." *College English*, vol. 78, no. 3, 2016, pp. 207–18.

Matsuda, Paul Kei. "The Myth of Linguistic Homogeneity in U.S. College Composition." *College English*, vol. 68, no. 6, 2006, pp. 637–51.

McLaren, Peter L. "On Ideology and Education: Critical Pedagogy and the Politics of Empowerment." *Social Text*, no. 19/20, 1988, pp. 153–85. *JSTOR*, www.jstor.org/stable/466183.

Medgyes, Peter. *The Non-native Teacher*. Macmillan, 1994.

Morrison, Toni. "Nobel Lecture." 7 Dec. 1993. *The Nobel Prize*, https://www.nobelprize.org/prizes/literature/1993/morrison/lecture/.

Office of Strategic Analysis and Reporting, UNT Dallas. "Fall 2015 Fact Sheet." University of North Texas at Dallas, https://sar.untdallas.edu/sites/default/files/factsheet_fa15.pdf.

Pavlenko, Aneta. "'I Never Knew I Was a Bilingual': Reimagining Teacher Identities in TESOL." *Journal of Language, Identity, and Education*, vol. 2, no. 4, 2003, pp. 251–68.

Ray, Brian. "'It's Beautiful': Language Difference as a New Norm in College Writing Instruction." *College Composition and Communication*, vol. 67, no. 1, 2015, pp. 87–103.

Sachs, Judyth. "Teacher Professional Identity: Competing Discourses, Competing Outcomes." *Journal of Education Policy*, vol. 16, no. 2, 2001, pp. 149–61.

CHAPTER SEVEN

Literacy, Rhetoric, Language Barriers, and Academia: A Journey of Knowledge and Identity

ESTEFANY PALACIO
Kennesaw State University

I am an academic in training. This idea had not dawned on me until just a couple of months ago, when I decided that a doctorate in rhetoric and composition will be the next step in my educational life. The decision to pursue a career in academia is one that trails back to my immigration story. If I had to write down a list of categories to describe myself, the following would be included: female, Latina, immigrant, scholar, writer, tech fanatic, and family oriented. These categories are simply the first items that came to mind, and they are also some of the most important factors that make me *me*. To enter the world of academia, one needs to have a desire for obtaining knowledge just as much as for creating knowledge. I desire to do both, and after living through a process of immigration that has led to a renewed relationship with language, I see migration and immigration as activities that can inform an approach to composition and communication through the different mediums and technologies available for creating and disseminating information.

Content creation and delivery practices are constantly evolving. As changes in technology have impacted my life, I have embraced them and welcomed them as part of my identity so that I can produce the best content possible, according to the availability of mediums and audience needs. My experiences with immigration, language, and communication have allowed me to perceive my identity as a hybrid state that incorporates different cultures, knowledges, and approaches to communication. To better illustrate the reasoning behind the identity categories I briefly mentioned, as well as my decision to become an academic, I discuss here my story of immigration, along with the influence of technology and rhetoric on my educational path to becoming an academic in the field of rhetoric and composition and my approach to communication as an act of migration between mediums of creation and delivery.

On Immigration to the United States and Exploring Identity

Being uprooted from my homeland was not my decision, but looking back, it was the right one. Immigration was the right turn at the right time, and it is something that has shaped my identity. Immigration is the backbone of the story of "me." Moving from Colombia to the United States was a catalyst for thoughts, decisions, and actions that have made me who I am today, not just as a Latina in the United States, but as a Latina who is looking to further her education in order to become a scholar. This decision to pursue a career in academia, specifically in rhetoric and composition, is not one that I made when I was young. I never dreamt of studying to become what many of my professors have become for me: mentors and guides for paths of inquiry, investigation, hypothesis making, and communication. I discovered my desire to pursue a path toward a life as a scholar of rhetoric and composition as a graduate student, and as I learn more and more about my field, I identify more opportunities to include my opinion and experiences, especially when I see that immigration and migration are not just physical acts.[1] They can also take place in composition and communication in general.

When I was eleven years old, my mother recognized that the financial situation in our home country of Colombia was not the best for a single mother, and she decided to make a change. Thanks to support from her brothers who were living in the United States, the next thing I knew I was an immigrant child in the state of Georgia. The process of immigration was fast-paced. My mother had already been in the United States for about a year,

Literacy, Rhetoric, Language Barriers, and Academia

and I had a visa, so once we decided that I would be moving, only a couple of days later I was traveling to the place I would now call home, a place where it would be easier to pursue my dreams. My mom wanted a better future for me, so once we arrived in the United States, she started to look for schools so that I could figure out the American world on my own terms. You see, education in Colombia is approached a bit differently than in the United States. In both public and private schools, for example, students are required to wear uniforms. Religion is also more central in the educational development of the students, as Catholics make up the majority of the Colombian population.[2] Overall, my education in Colombia was excellent. I was exposed to a great variety of school subjects at an early age, which truly benefited my academic development. I was well prepared academically for my move to the United States, but not socially or linguistically.

Interactions among individuals in Colombia are highly influenced by the surroundings: sidewalks and public buses, churches and cafés, corner stores and bakeries, supermarkets and parks. The list goes on, but the point is that places act as platforms where conversations take place, where orality is present. When I lived in Colombia, I used to walk to school. Sometimes I would stop by the corner store to buy some snacks for recess, or stop by the bakery to pick up a freshly baked guava pastry. I would also attend church service on Sunday with my mom. All of these activities included talking to people at the store, visiting with the baker, and repeating my prayers in church. In the United States, I no longer performed many of these activities, in which Spanish was my main mode of communication. Because my mother knew I would struggle with English and with my social life once I moved to the United States, she ensured that I was registered in school right away so that I could begin to socialize, meet new people, and, of course, learn English. Through perseverance and my love for learning, I began to subdue my attachment to Colombia and to embrace my new home country.

Keeping my attachment to Colombia as muted as possible was important because any and all thoughts of Colombia would have acted as roadblocks in the development of my new identity, which was being shaped by a new home, a new school, a new culture, and a new language. I began sixth grade at a school comprising mostly American students. At that time, I defined *American* as someone born in the United States, White or African American, with English as their only or main language. I was enrolled in math, science, social studies, and language arts. I was also enrolled in ESL classes and learned English by the end of the school year. As a newly developed multilingual, I felt more comfortable interpreting dialogue because I could rely on the physical and the social environments for context (Canagarajah 19). I was removed from ESL classes at the end of sixth grade, so going into seventh grade I was more autonomous when it came to the ability to communicate with others, but I needed help with reading comprehension. I was assigned to a reading class where, through the use of silent reading and group reading as well as activities and group discussion, I increased my reading level. As a result, I was no longer restricted to only one wall of the library, where the only books I could initially read were located. Now I could walk around to other walls and sections of the library and read a greater variety of books. In addition to reading books on a regular basis, I began to interact more with computers. At the start of my US education, a reading comprehension quiz accompanied every book I read for school, and the quizzes took place on the computer. I also took a computer class elective that provided me more time in front of a computer monitor and with programs I had never before interacted with, such as animation and website-making applications.

During my middle school years, I wasn't as digitally savvy as I am today. I consider myself a digital immigrant (Prensky, "Digital Natives" 1) because although I grew up around the television, the radio, and the phone, digital technologies that could have had a deeper impact on my digital knowledge and communication practices, such as computers, tablets, digital cameras, and digital software, were not as common in my life until I moved to the United States. Immigrating to the United States also meant immigrating to a new way of approaching communication through digital means and a way for me to better adapt to my changing world. In the States, I began to spend more time with computers in school because of the reading tests and working in computer science class. Later on, I became more comfortable performing communication tasks using a computer and even created my first email and signed up for an MSN chat account. Thus began my experimentation with multimodality (Kress).

Looking back at my early interactions with technology, I can now see that digital media and rhetorical studies would inevitably cross my path one day. In high school, I was part of the yearbook staff. I began as a staff member during my junior year, in charge of developing my own story, everything from conducting research, to writing the story, to obtaining pictures, to adding all of that information into a template assigned by the editor-in-chief. By senior year, I was a coeditor-in-chief and therefore more involved with the development of the final product. Developing the yearbook's theme, creating templates, and editing the stories that other staff turned in were part of my job. Because yearbook was a class, I learned about photography and publishing guidelines. I was being exposed to visual rhetoric and was employing rhetorical appeals successfully, even though I wasn't aware of the terminology or theories at the time. I was, however, more aware of how images, just as much as words, present meaning and affect audiences.

During the second half of high school, I became more interested in how digital communications work. Thanks to my interaction with publishing software and with the yearbook class in general, I was aware of different approaches to communication and felt comfortable interacting with digital technologies. I perceived the presentation of visuals as structured and affective communication. I also, for the first time, understood writing as communication that can be successfully presented in different formats, depending on the needs of the audience. The concept of digital rhetoric and multimodality wasn't yet part of my mindset, but I definitely continued to work with multimodal forms of content delivery, such as electronic essays, emails, class discussions via Blackboard, PowerPoint presentations, and some video. Interacting with digital media as part of my high school education certainly left me eager to explore different approaches to communication, and, in retrospect, may have been an early influence on my eventual interest in rhetoric and communication. By the time I was ready for college, digital technology was part of my everyday communication practices, and very early in my college career I began to connect communication theories with my own approach to communication.

I enrolled in college with an "undecided" major but set on an academic path during my first year via English 1101, in which the professor discussed the three main rhetorical appeals. That was the moment when I decided to pursue English as my major. Like Lizbett Tinoco's choice to pursue a degree in English to better understand the power of language (this volume), I couldn't ignore the importance of understanding the components of an argument, how the knowledge and credibility of a writer affects the opinion of the reader, as well as the emotions evoked by the words and the content itself. When I lived in Colombia, I was young and simply trying to understand language and its workings in Spanish. I wasn't aware of how arguments are shaped. I didn't understand the makings of a successful message or the reasons why certain content has an emotional impact on me, or the influences behind the author's choice to present content one way over another. Being exposed to rhetorical appeals in that introductory English class helped me understand that knowledge about language is extremely valuable and forever useful. That class also let me know that I was experiencing only a brief introduction to a field that could guide me to an understanding of the power of communication, as developed through different approaches and views. In my early years in the United States, as a young immigrant, I was still developing my vocabulary and language practices in Spanish. Leaving that linguistic place of comfort and adapting to a new language allowed me to appreciate communication more fully. My new understanding of rhetoric and the theoretical workings of communication let me see what someone like me, an individual with a hybrid identity, could do with language. I knew that Aristotle's discussions were profound and influential on today's communication practices, but I wanted to learn more, to understand how some of the greatest writers and theorists made connections with their readers, as well as how readers end up reading specific writers. I knew that many challenges awaited me, mainly because I had chosen English as my major even though English is my second language. I was nervous about my lack of familiarity with theories and concepts that were common to other students. I was also afraid of not being able to understand certain authors' approaches to content within different genres, since sayings and idioms vary from place to place, culture to culture, and language to language. Nonetheless, I welcomed the challenges and embraced the good and the bad that came from pursuing an English degree as an immigrant and nonnative English speaker.

As an undergraduate English major, I decided to focus specifically on rhetoric and composition. My writing was and still is all right. It's always a process of trial and error, of following the rules of grammar, or of crafting clever arguments to support the decision to not follow them.[3] Fortunately, theories and approaches to writing are flexible. Through understanding theory and rhetorical approaches, I learned that I could control my writing, shape it, and have a specific purpose and audience. This was the first time that I truly understood the different layers that constitute writing. I began to see that, depending on the goal of my writing, I can decide or control how much information I provide or keep from my audience and how I want to present information. Through different literature courses and elective classes like anthropology, I became more aware of my differences compared to those around me. This awareness was part of the calling to continue my education in the field of writing. I was different, and though that might not have been immediately obvious, that difference could be heard in my accent and noticed in my attitude. I didn't choose writing and rhetoric simply to learn about approaches to writing, but rather to be part of a conversation and to challenge points of view. Between my different worlds—student, immigrant, writer and rhetorician in training—I have encountered opportunities to explore different means of communication, and my hybrid identity helps me to be analytical yet open to opinions and theories.

My immigration story has had a major influence on the way I think, speak, and migrate between communication practices. As an immigrant child who had no choice but to move to a different country, a country that was always presented as a place of dreamers and liberties, I knew that I had to follow those dreams and enjoy the liberties. So I began my process of acculturation, moved on to pursue a college degree, then graduate school, and currently am reflecting on my own story and its influence on my professional decisions, including my communication practices. Through acculturation, I modified my original identity by immersing myself in a new culture, with new forms of entertainment, including watching television shows in English and interacting with English-speaking individuals. As I matured, I became aware of the development of my American culture and my ability to navigate my new biculturalism (Bacallao and Smokowski 146). When communicating, I have embraced my hybrid identity and employ code switching to move from Spanish to English, and vice versa, depending on the situation.

I didn't recognize the value of different forms of communication until I began to study rhetoric, and I haven't stopped since. Looking back, there is a network across two worlds that has helped shape who I am today. Much from my upbringing still connects to my present-day communication practices. I come from a country where communication is loud and colorful. Colombians make great use of orality. Songs, hymns, and prayers helped me learn about historical moments, religion, and common beliefs. Recipes are still passed down through demonstration, not necessarily through a recipe card. Part of Colombian folklore includes stories about mythical creatures that live in rural areas. I heard many of these growing up when we spent our weekends at our *finca*, or country home. Orality is evident in the many conversations that take place at the lunch hour dining table, in the sermon from the daily mass, in the street vendors who loudly advertise their products, in friends sharing a cup of coffee in cafés, and in the ubiquitous presence of house phone lines that allow family members to communicate daily. Literacy is also widespread; most of the population is literate.[4] Culturally, verbal communication is still the preferred mode of interaction among individuals. My family and I have always held conversations at the dining table. Our family table has generated business ideas, solutions to arguments, and so on. This activity hasn't changed since my move to the United States. At my dining table here in the States I have sat down to work on homework and to prepare for classes. At this dining table I read Gloria Anzaldúa's "How to Tame a Wild Tongue," a story that changed my life forever, as well as my outlook on communication, rhetoric, and everything in between.

"How to Tame a Wild Tongue," a story of identity, was the first story I encountered that made me think about my own identity. Prior to college, I simply saw myself as a persevering human being trying to survive in society. I didn't read much into my differences, because I kept them minimized by acculturating. Reading Anzaldúa's work, however, was my hailing[5] moment, when I realized that I was part of a bigger story (Althusser 190). While diverse families like Anzaldúa's are common in the United States, their commitment to perseverance is so strong that immigrants often work hard to forget their roots and accommodate to the norm. Anzaldúa describes how she didn't fit in either of her countries' cultures. Hers was a "borderline" identity, one that shared aspects of both Mexico and the United States, from taste in music, to food choices, to the way she spoke depending on the person listening. Code switching was part of Anzaldúa's communication behavior. As a Chicana, Anzaldúa spoke a certain way; as a scholar, she spoke another way; as an American, she had a different voice; and as a Mexican, she communicated in yet a different way. Code switching is a reflection of identity and a physical representation of the presence of more than one culture in an individual's life.[6] Deciding when to speak a language is a skill gained after spending time between borders. According to Anzaldúa:

> For a people who are neither Spanish nor live in a country in which Spanish is the first language; for a people who live in a country in which English is the reigning tongue but who are not Anglo; for a people who cannot entirely identify with either standard (formal, Castilian) Spanish nor standard English, what recourse is left but to create their own language? A language which they can connect their identity to, one capable of communicating the realities and values true to themselves—a language—with terms that are neither *español ni inglés*, but both. We speak a patois, a forked tongue, a variation of two languages. (77)

The variations in languages brings to the speaker an awareness of audience that in cases like Anzaldúa's, and mine, is helpful in the field of rhetoric and composition. I identify so much with Anzaldúa's struggle to find a voice, an identity, especially coming from a place where orality in Spanish was a major part of my life to my new home, where I wasn't able to count on orality because of my lack of English. Her discussion of a "borderland identity" is probably one of the greatest arguments I have read, because I can see myself as someone whose identity is in an in-between place. I have officially lived in the United States more than half of my life. I may not look too different, but my Spanish accent comes out at times. Still, I am American. I have been going through the process of acculturation since day one. Through this process, I have modified my own culture due to my contact with a new one (Amaya 198). I have embraced the language, the slang, the food, the clothes, and the music. I have legally changed my nationality by becoming a naturalized US citizen; there's a certificate with my picture as proof of the legal process. And, while that piece of paper holds so much power over my decisions, my benefits, my life, and my future, there was another piece of paper in existence before the certificate of naturalization—my birth certificate. That piece of paper takes me back to the place where I was born, a place completely different from this one. Becoming a naturalized citizen was the ultimate act of acculturation. I decided to fully immerse myself in the United States through an official, legal process in order to enjoy legal benefits such as voting and knowing that I can live in the States and visit Colombia. Two different pieces of paper tell me who I am.[7] Not *"Ni de aquí, ni de allá,"* "not from here, not from there," but *"de aquí y de allá,"* "from here and from there." I am indeed from both places, and it took quite a while to understand that. I have a hybrid identity. Most of the time, both sides of the border are present in my decisions and my work, and, recognizing that I am from two places, one that birthed me and another that raised me, has led me to change the way I view and understand communication.

Communication has been changing and morphing to comply with or adapt to whatever influential factors are behind the changes. The act of communication is one that comes naturally to humanity. It started with orality and the need to share information, then came literacy and the need to record such information, and now with "electracy" (Ulmer), the process of creating and disseminating information is taking many shapes, including digital works. As my knowledge about writing and rhetoric has increased, I have also been able to better understand my relationship with communication and how my immigration story influences it. By framing communication as an act of migration between modes of content creation and delivery in order to successfully present information, I can decide when to employ each aspect of communication, an approach that can be applied by any communicator, regardless of personal experience. Each type of discourse—oral, literate, and electrate—is best employed under specific conditions, and those specific conditions will be determined by the rhetorical situation.

- **Orality.** Orality is an essential part of my life. As I mentioned earlier, the dining table was where my family shared many conversations. At a very young age, I was encouraged to memorize material. I learned my city's anthem for the monthly flag celebration at school. I learned all of my prayers for church and the religious celebrations that took place every year, and even before I knew all of the different prayers, I had memorized the letters of the alphabet through song. The music that I still enjoy contains messages, some positive, some with social commentary, others simply telling a love story, and so on. Secondary orality, that which is sustained by electronic devices like television and radio (Ong, *Orality* 11), has always been and will always be an important aspect of my life. Orality is evolving and being reshaped through technological advances and cultural changes such as podcasts and videos. Through the study of rhetoric and composition, writers and content creators can use orality as one of the vehicles of delivery, alongside other forms such as image and text, to create content that showcases the hybridity of our society's communication practices.

- **Literacy.** Literacy, the ability to read and write, begins at an early age. Elementary school required me to quickly learn to identify the many letters of the Spanish alphabet, their sounds and sound combinations, how to write them, and their meanings when put together. With Spanish, the writing process is quite simple because there aren't many letter combinations and the letter sounds are unique, making them easy to recognize. You can sound out a word and know if you need two *r*'s or if you need an *ñ*. You can also know whether a word requires a *v* or a *b* and so on. Learning Spanish was for me an act of orality. I first heard the language and later learned to write it. Learning English, however, was a mix of orality and literacy. In English, spelling and pronunciation are a bit more difficult. I still remember my surprise when I noticed that *telephone* had a *ph* instead of an *f* and that the name *Steven* could also be spelled *Stephen* and yet sound the same. Pre-immigration, I was used to one way of speaking and writing, and I couldn't understand why in English there had to be two letters in the word (*ph*) when one could make the same sound (*f*). Phonetic differences were hard to understand when I was learning English, and this was because I was already literate in the Spanish alphabet. Because the alphabets in both languages are so similar, I always pictured a word combination when someone spoke to me in English. According to Walter J. Ong, we visualize words when we hear them because we have interiorized the technology of writing ("Writing" 294). The ability to recognize linguistic differences when reading is one of the most helpful skills I have acquired over the years.

◆ **Electracy.** I was not aware of what electracy was until I encountered a discussion about it in graduate school. Gregory L. Ulmer says that electracy "does not already exist as such, but names an apparatus that is emerging 'as we speak,' rising in many different spheres and areas, and converging in some unforeseeable yet malleable way" (7). Electracy is a bridge between different approaches to language and communication, bringing them together. Living in Colombia, I was accustomed to communicating verbally, through conversations, phone calls, church services, and other situations that called for verbal communication. Once in the United States, the process of acculturation was made possible by my interaction with literacy. To learn English, I had to practice reading and writing in the new language. Today, with electracy, I combine orality and literacy as I communicate through digital mediums such as electronic text, video, and audio. My identity has had a chance to explore its hybridity in a closer manner thanks to the different options for communication that electracy presents.

Ulmer discusses electracy as a response to our everyday surroundings. Our careers, families, modes of entertainment, and community drive our interactions with technologies and communication practices that go beyond speaking and writing. In my case, electracy has been present in my life since I have been able to use a computer and my computer literacy skills to enhance my communication practices. We now use emails, text messages, phone calls, video calls, and much more to remain connected. The age of electracy is an enhanced secondary orality in which there is still a participatory mystique and communal sensibility (Ong, *Orality* 136), one that doesn't require in-person interaction but can take place through a screen, a set of headphones, etc. Electracy takes orality and literacy to a new level because it's a hybrid of the two. In the field of academia, instruction style and class content can be positively influenced by the combination of orality, literacy, and technology. Examples of electracy in the way college classes are designed are multiplying rapidly. Communication between students and instructors takes place via email as much as in person. Assignments take different forms of delivery, including videos and presentations. Some classes take place online, where all interaction between students and instructors is digital. While digital spaces may take the face-to-face interaction out of the equation, communicators still have to work hard to ensure that the content being presented is well developed, makes proper use of the technology, and provides a positive user experience.

Technology Is Everywhere: The Mix of Orality, Literacy, and Technology

Currently, I am in the process of learning and absorbing as much information as I can about the field of rhetoric, composition, and professional writing. As a communicator, I have recognized the influence my hybrid identity has had on my approach to communication. Now that I'm aware of the connection between orality, literacy, and technology, writing has become a much more rhetorically successful task because I have more options for presenting content. Overall, my communication practices have changed greatly due to the presence of technology in my life. With orality, I'm able to maintain conversations in two different languages. I also code switch to better adapt to each rhetorical situation. With literacy and electracy, I migrate between mediums of content creation and content delivery—a kind of code switching—to ensure that I present my work in the most appropriate manner for my audience.

The computer is currently my main mode of content creation. The need for a digital device occurred during my undergraduate studies. All of the courses that required written work also required it in electronic form. Other than some PowerPoint presentations and digital projects for my college-level computer course, I mostly used Microsoft Word to create content. As a graduate student, however, I began to see communication as something more intricate and experimental. Through different projects and opportunities outside of the classroom, I have been able to migrate between modes of content creation and delivery to share my knowledge about different technologies and how they impact my communication practices. I have presented content through slides, videos, audio recordings, and essays, and I have had great conversations about communication practices, including multicultural perspectives.

Code switching has become more than a consequence of ongoing adaptation to change. Code switching is a determinant of identity. The fact that I constantly "travel" or "migrate" from Spanish to English, and vice versa, indicates that my identity is still in development and not absolutely defined. I adapt my language to each and every communication situation, and realizing this helps me see the vast opportunities I have to connect with audiences simply because I'm able to adapt to different language environments. Regardless of the number of languages a person speaks, however, code switching is also a phenomenon within a single language. In addition to dialect differences, codes vary according to each rhetorical situation. For example, students of rhetoric and composition communicate in a more academic code in class than they do with friends who pursue other academic endeavors. It's important for communicators to understand that code switching is part of their identities, and the sooner this happens, the more rhetorically successful their conversations will be.

I have embraced code switching and fully believe in my approach to communication as an act of migration. Therefore, the desire to be able to check a specific box on a form in order to identify myself is gone, and questions have replaced that desire. Who is Estefany Palacio? Such a question truly has no specific answer, but I can provide some clues and specific categories. I am a female, an immigrant, a graduate student, and a writer (who embraces both the traditional form of writing as well as digital forms). These descriptions are accurate. One of them specifically, immigrant, has led to the presence of other defining characteristics in my life such as being bilingual and being a graduate student. Bilingualism was a necessary change in my life in order for me to properly acculturate to the United States. Graduate school, however, was not so much part of the acculturation process as a result of it. Once embarked on my college career, I realized that I had the opportunity to continue studying and increasing my knowledge of the field of rhetoric and composition. Immigration

Literacy, Rhetoric, Language Barriers, and Academia

has also made me a migrant. While I didn't have much choice about moving to the United States, and while this move was permanent, I do get to return to Colombia as a visitor. I also migrate between languages depending on the place where I am and the audience. Furthermore, my exposure to the world of academia, including the different types of research I have done for projects and my own experiences and analysis of my situation, has led me to recognize another type of migration taking place in my life, and it's due to my interaction with technology.

It goes without saying that in writing and composition, one needs to be aware of audience. Along with the content, audience awareness has a big influence on the medium of delivery. After experimenting with different forms of content delivery and content creation, I have realized that choosing between creation options and between delivery options is a kind of migration. Perceiving content creation and delivery as acts of migration is a good way for writers and other content creators to understand the different possibilities available to them when creating and sharing content. Approaching writing and publication as migration is a more conscious, optional, and impermanent act, allowing the communicator to deliberately evaluate the audience so that content is presented in the most appropriate medium of delivery. If the content needs to take a different format for whatever reason, the change, or migratory action, is a conscious, well-thought-out one.

The society that surrounds me and that will likely be my most frequent audience (future college students) is the constant target of advertisements to be part of a technological era by purchasing gadgets and software designed to increase productivity and organization both at work and at home, and to enhance entertainment experiences. Information can be presented through so many different mediums, and younger generations are comfortable with digital content delivery, embracing their presence and use. More people are obtaining their news from websites and through social media platforms. Looking to Google for help with any question is common among Internet users, and entertainment is more than ever taking place through digital means and technological gadgets. These changes in society due to the prevalence of technology make my job as a writer and future educator one of finding the best means of communication in order to provide digital wisdom (Prensky, *Brain Gain* 203) and to inform and educate the masses.

Graduate classrooms are a great place to have conversations about migration between modes of content creation and content delivery. Let me elaborate. I have taken the seminar/conversational/open forum style of the graduate course and, where possible, migrated that approach to my final projects through digital works that move way beyond the everyday academic essay. One example is a digital magazine I created for my Technical Writing course, designed on a digital publishing platform that housed the tools for editing content. Because of the digital nature of the magazine and the platform that hosted it, I was able to include a video that served as the "editor's note." I was also able to hyperlink every item in the table of contents to each specific page and include images and color to enhance the written content. The articles included discussion and analysis of different essays on the cognizance of audience throughout the writing process. My choice to migrate from a regular essay to a magazine was driven by the course as much as by the audience—students and an instructor who embrace digital media. I enjoyed learning the software and interacting with the publishing platform. The creation process of the project wasn't easy, and the technology had its learning curve. Regardless, the project's final version looked impressive and stands as a great example of my migration between mediums, as well as the migration taking place in the publishing world. Although the magazine was digital, the reader was able to "flip" the pages by clicking on the arrow, which produced the sound of a physical page being turned.

Being able to create projects like a digital magazine provides writers the opportunity to reach more individuals, especially the increasing number of digital natives who enjoy learning through digital means and are more open to the idea of digital classroom materials and even classroom spaces. Moreover, participation through electracy brings about an interesting dynamic in which creators can also be teachers and students can be archivists (Arroyo 8). Electracy offers the opportunity to present intellectual knowledge in a nontraditional way. What's great about this approach is that digital projects don't have to be the answer to all communication tasks; they are simply another option.

Conclusion: It's All an Everlasting Cycle

Acculturation for me proved to be a good approach to my life post-immigration. As a hybrid individual, one who embraces her Colombian roots yet feels very American, I have placed significant value in the way language and language practices connect us. The field of rhetoric and composition has allowed me a space where I can play with language and mediums to ensure that I create the best content possible. Life has certainly thrown me some challenges. In my first months in the United States, I was desperate to belong. All I wanted to do was understand my peers and interact through conversation as I had done in my homeland, but I couldn't. Time went by and I learned English, made friends, learned about US culture, and began to feel more American.

Only when I left high school did I realize that being American isn't easy to define. After turning eighteen, I had to legally reject my Colombian nationality and become a naturalized citizen of the United States. Up to that point, I had considered the official, legal change as a way of being American. The thing is, when you have lived in different countries, spoken two different languages, and experienced two different cultures, it's hard to immediately pick—or even distinguish—one identity. During my junior and senior years of college, I began to read authors like Anzaldúa, who showed me that identity is a much more complicated issue than being the citizen of a country. Anzaldúa was the first author to show me the struggle behind the quest to define one's position in a bicultural, bilingual, and overall diverse world. Now that I have authors like Anzaldúa to guide me, along with my embrace of digital media, I feel I can narrow down my identity a little more. I have accepted the fact that there is not one specific "side" to identity. I have a place in society that is waiting for me as a future instructor in a field that has opened doors of inquiry and has allowed me in. I have a new outlook on communication and communication practices. Along with embracing digital media and content creation, I will be able to shape my teaching style and knowledge to fit the future audiences of academia—digital natives.

In this new, electrate world, communication is facing a state of hybridity in which orality and literacy have come together with digital technology to create a new stage in the world of communication, changing communication practices forever. Writing and reading take different forms and provide users with different experiences. Likewise, the act of writing is evolving, taking on new terms like *content creation* and adapting to new mediums of presentation. Rhetorically speaking, the hybridity of electracy allows communicators to choose specific modes of delivery to successfully communicate with audiences. A good way of understanding the value of such hybridity in communication is through the metaphor of migration: content creators migrate between mediums, including paper, screen, voice, video, and more, to present their information via the best platform possible, enhancing the potential for a successful rhetorical act.

Notes

1. See Jeff Rice's *Digital Detroit: Rhetoric and Space in the Age of Network*. Through his outlook on Detroit, Rice presents a city as a place that comprises more than the actions of the individuals living there. Rhetorically speaking, the city is a network, and the many references Rice mentions are part of that network. Navigating the city is not only a physical act, but also a virtual experience as information is presented not only through street signs and roads, but also through maps and navigation applications. Similarly, my conception of migration as something beyond a physical act involves drawing a parallel between the choice to move from one place to another and the choice to move from one medium of communication to another during content creation and delivery.

2. According to the CIA World Factbook, the Roman Catholic population of Colombia is 79 percent ("World Factbook").

3. See Martha Kolln's *Rhetorical Grammar: Grammatical Choices, Rhetorical Effects*, which presents an approach to grammar that allows readers to think about the reasoning behind their grammatical decisions. The content covers the rules and the grammatical regulations behind successful writing while honoring a writer's own approach to content.

4. According to the CIA World Factbook, the literacy rate of Colombia is 94.7 percent ("World Factbook").

5. For Althusser, being "hailed" is part of the act of interpellation, in which "ideology acts or functions in such a way as to recruit subjects

among individuals or transform individuals into subjects" (190). We are called into being, or identifying with a certain situation, that in turn influences our identity.

6. See Victor Villanueva's *Bootstraps: From an American Academic of Color*. Code switching can be seen as rhetorical power because the meaning of words isn't fixed, allowing the speaker to emphasize a concept through a specific term or choice of language. As a bilingual individual, when I'm reading in English and there are Spanish words in the text, I rhetorically decide to pronounce the Spanish words as I would in Spanish to emphasize their meaning and influence in the conversation.

7. See Kate Vieira's *American by Paper: How Documents Matter in Immigrant Literacy*. Stories similar to mine are presented, such as that of Cristina (72), a woman who saw a change in her identity as soon as she was able to obtain "papers." From a visa to a residence card to a certificate of naturalization, "papers" have always had a strong influence in the lives of immigrants. These pieces of paper are not only tangible proof of a legal status, but also symbols of a new identity.

Works Cited

Althusser, Louis. *On the Reproduction of Capitalism: Ideology and Ideological State Apparatuses*. Verso, 2014.

Amaya, Hector. "Performing Acculturation: Rewriting the Latina/o Immigrant Self." *Text and Performance Quarterly*, vol. 27, no. 3, 2007, pp. 194–212.

Anzaldúa, Gloria. "How to Tame a Wild Tongue." *Borderlands = La Frontera: the New Mestiza*, Aunt Lute Books, 2012.

Arroyo, Sarah J. *Participatory Composition: Video Culture, Writing, and Electracy*. Southern Illinois UP, 2013.

Bacallao, Martica, and Paul R. Smokowski. "Worlds Apart: Bicultural Identity Development in Latino Adolescents." *Acculturation: Implications for Individuals, Families and Societies*, edited by Tara M. Johnson, Nova Science Publishers, 2011, pp. 133–49.

Canagarajah, Suresh. "Multilingual Strategies of Negotiating English: From Conversation to Writing." *JAC: A Journal of Composition Theory*, vol. 29, no. 1, 2009, pp. 17–48.

Kolln, Martha. *Rhetorical Grammar: Grammatical Choices, Rhetorical Effects*. Longman, 2002.

Kress, Gunther R. *Literacy in the New Media Age.* Routledge, 2003.

Ong, Walter J. *Orality and Literacy: The Technologizing of the Word.* Routledge, 2007.

———. "Writing Is a Technology That Restructures Thought." *The Linguistics of Literacy,* edited by Pamela Downing et al., John Benjamins, 1992, pp. 293–320.

Prensky, Marc. *Brain Gain: Technology and the Quest for Digital Wisdom.* Palgrave Macmillan, 2012.

———. "Digital Natives, Digital Immigrants." *On the Horizon: The Strategic Planning Resource for Education Professionals,* vol. 9, no. 5, 2001, pp. 1–6.

Rice, Jeff. *Digital Detroit: Rhetoric and Space in the Age of the Network.* Southern Illinois UP, 2012.

Ulmer, Gregory L. *Internet Invention: From Literacy to Electracy.* Pearson Higher Education, 2003.

Vieira, Kate. *American by Paper: How Documents Matter in Immigrant Literacy.* U of Minnesota P, 2016.

Villanueva, Victor, Jr. *Bootstraps: From an American Academic of Color.* National Council of Teachers of English, 1993.

"The World Factbook: Colombia." *Central Intelligence Agency,* 1 Feb. 2018, https://www.cia.gov/library/publications/resources/the-world-factbook/geos/co.html.

CHAPTER EIGHT

From Orality to Electracy: A Mystory

SERGIO C. FIGUEIREDO
Kennesaw State University

I have always had a conflicted relationship with the academy. Like other multilingual immigrant scholars (Anzaldúa; Villanueva; those collected in this volume), the academy's use of literacy has always felt like a "navigational technology that opens up some paths and closes off others, that orients and disorients, that routes and reroutes" (Vieira, "On the Social" 27), and that limits the potential of inventive, experimental, and nonstandard composition practices that allow one to resist the interpellation function of institutional literacies (cf. Vieira, *American* 7). Like the young people that Kate Vieira describes in *American by Paper*, my experiences with literacy in the academy were managerial and regulatory. And, like the undocumented college student, Simone, Vieira interviews about the role of literacy in young immigrants' lives, the most meaningful college writing projects I composed were multimodal ones that allowed me to break away from literacy's role in maintaining the authority of the academy (*American* 135); institutional literacies were (are?) simply about passing and passage, a tool of a disciplinary society.

In fact, it was my first experience with academic literacy (as a disciplinary tool) that has informed my scholarly interests in rhetorical invention, "new" media, and experimental composition practices. As a member of the first generation of my family born in the United States and as a first-generation college student, I was already unsure about my ability to succeed in a university setting when I entered my first class in September 2001: first-year composition. To make matters more tumultuous, a week into class the Twin Towers were hit by airplanes, just a few hours' drive up the New Jersey turnpike, near where my extended family was living. We learned of these attacks when our FYC teacher entered the classroom promptly at 9:00 a.m. and turned on the television. Less than ten minutes later, the instructor turned off the screen and got back to the work of the day, preparing first-year students to write in the ways the academy expected. Expectations that did not allow us (students) opportunities to deal with our own immediate needs. Despite having met all of these expectations, the instructor told me at the end of the term that I should consider retaking the course because she did not believe I was prepared to take the second course in the sequence. A second instructor participating in FYC assessment disagreed with the first about my readiness to move forward.

The dissonance of this experience would later come to define the central problems composition studies scholars would soon identify in critical and process-based pedagogy. For instance, earlier that year, Thomas Rickert critiqued the field along similar lines and identified a new course of action:

> The next step for writing pedagogy . . . cannot be that we just stop teaching writing as we have been teaching it. Given the institutional fetishization of thesis statements, grades, and grammar, this would be nearly impossible anyway. Instead, we might infuse own particular pedagogies with this insight into education's general culpability, to the extent that we grant students the possibilities for a writing that would be . . . their own "act." This approach asks us to acknowledge that we do not always know best how to rectify social problems for them, and this further necessitates that we partially relinquish control to, and learn from, students. ("'Hands Up'" 291)

The following year, Geoff Sirc would make a similar claim, arguing that "we" (composition teachers) "build our Museums, peculiar sorts of cultural temples in which students are 'invited' in to sample the best that has been thought and expressed in *our language* and maybe even . . . to learn to reproduce the master's craft" (2, original emphasis). Like Quentin Pierce, the student in David Bartholomae's "The Tidy House" in *Writing on the Margins* (which both Rickert and Sirc reference), my first experience with the academy's language was one of detachment, disengagement. I (alongside other young Generation 1.5 and second-generation immigrants Vieira describes in *American by Paper*)[1] had little interest in assimilating to the kind of institutionalized literacies that function as technologies of decontextualization, oppression, and alienation (Vieira, *American* 146). However, it would take almost a decade, interspersed with other events that emphasized this sense of detachment and disengagement, before I would be able to understand my experience in terms of the problems associated with the function of literacy as a process of social and cultural assimilation.

My understanding of this experience of literacy came only during my first year in Clemson University's rhetoric, communication, and information design doctoral program, and specifically in Victor Vitanza's courses, Histories of Rhetorics[2] and Cultural Research Methods, and through a dissertation on composition theory and pedagogy under the direction of Cynthia Haynes.[3] Reading Eric Havelock's *The Muse Learns to Write*, Walter Ong's *Orality & Literacy*, and Gregory Ulmer's *Heuretics* and *Internet Invention* (among other of Ulmer's books) revealed to me the problems of my first experience with the academy: the pedagogy of literacy as practiced in the university was one that emphasizes what Sarah Arroyo calls the "discourse of mastery" (*Participatory Composition* 111). What struck me most about this scholarship was how it helped me to understand my family's communication practices. Like Arroyo, I came across these concepts as I was "playing around with ideas and concepts, looking for my place in the discipline of rhetoric and composition, and crawling through the theories and practices of my mentors" ("Growing Up"), learning about the institutional, pedagogical, and ideological implications of Ulmer's work on *electracy*—an updated and theoretically fleshed-out version of Ong's "secondary orality" (*Orality*). And there it was, an epiphany: I was (am) *electrate*. I did (do) not fit into the *literate* institution.[4] My parents were a part of the first generation in their families to have access to *literacy*, access my mother would later use to write a letter to an uncle living in the United States that would eventually lead to our family's legal passage into the country.[5] My first experience in school was access to computer technology, which would come to offer opportunities to reach back across the Atlantic Ocean to connect with family still living in Europe. In three generations, my family's discourse practices shifted from orality to literacy to electracy. When I entered the (literate) academy, I did not feel the distress most literates did about nonstandard language use, what Ong describes as the unfulfilled desire to have "words and thoughts pinned down"; I was at home in thinking of language in the manner of primary orality, as "an event, a happening, not a thing, as letters make it appear to be" ("Writing" 25). From my grandparents, who did not know how to read or write, and my parents, I learned to experience language (spoken and written) as a series of events.

What led to this epiphany was an education reflecting the kind of rhetorical sensibility Juan C. Guerra identifies as a *translingual* approach that develops in students a "critical awareness of language as a contingent and emergent, rather than standardized and static, practice" (228) and its intersection with Jody Shipka's call for the field to consider, through the concept of *transmodality*,

> how concretely engaging with different modes, genres, materials, cultural practices, communicative technologies, and language varieties impacts our abilities to make and negotiate meaning, how it impacts both what we know and how we come to know, and perhaps most importantly, how it might provide us with still other options for knowing and being, and for being known. (251)

Shipka's is an approach grounded in theories of postpedagogy and postprocess pedagogy wherein students' communication practices are treated as particulars, as non-standard and non-static *happenings*,[6] with one overarching goal: each student should reflect on how their respective rhetorical choices in a given (mediated) communication act either enhances or detracts from the particular communication goals of that act. As Shipka describes it, this would be an approach that encourages an "enriched awareness" about our (and our students') communication practices and is accomplished

> by asking students (and asking ourselves) to consider the range of conventions, technologies, materials, and practices they (we)

typically encounter in different areas or domains—at school, in the workplace, at home, in places of worship, while shopping, while communicating online or face-to-face, and so on. (255)

In fact, it is this exact kind of approach that led to my own epiphany, and it is one that I have taught using the network-theory inspired genre that Ulmer invented in *Internet Invention*, the *mystory*.[7]

As Marc Santos and colleagues explain, the mystory genre aims to create "aha moments" that function not in terms of "pedagogical mastery but of pedagogical serendipity." As others in this collection (Guglielmo; Mayshle; Palacio) have suggested, the desire to foster mastery in our students (who may one day become our colleagues) is a point of contention for many American immigrant scholars; the emphasis, in many ways, requires that we ignore the range of conventions, technologies, materials, and institutional practices that we have learned to merge as we adapt to new institutions (and their practices) in favor of assimilating to (mastering) the conventions of the dominant system (ideology). To encourage these sorts of epiphanies, I propose that research in the field of translanguaging develop hybridized and integrated communication systems using Shipka's theoretical framework of transmodality as an entry point. In what follows, I offer a mystory as a performance of how this genre/method[8] led to my own epiphany—how my multicultural, multilingual, and multimodal experiences have informed my scholarly and pedagogical work. Following Ulmer's assignment, I begin by documenting a key invention in my home field (rhetoric) before exploring how the roles played by my familial (Portuguese), entertainment (digital technologies), and community (Luso-Americans and rhetoricians) discourse practices have influenced my work.

Mystory

At the heart of the mystory genre is a tradition of humanities wisdom: know thyself (Ulmer, *Internet* xiii). As a genre designed for the emerging era of electracy, "its most significant impact concerns how . . . new forms of expression help reconceptualize the human otherwise than the Cartesian, individuated *self* central to literacy's logocentric forms of thinking/doubting reasoning" and augments literacy's "emphasis on logic and reason with a sophisticated appreciation of feeling and affect" (Santos et al., para. 1). In place of *self*, the mystory positions the author of the genre as part of a collective network of associations; in a later work, Ulmer calls this new identity practice *avatar*, a term derived from videogame discourse meant to describe a person who is "always at work within a larger system yet retains the ability to change that system" (Santos et al., para. 3).[9] In the context of translingualism and transmodality, this theoretical framework would acknowledge that first-generation immigrants and the children of immigrants are not defined by a singular identity—that of our immigrant status—but instead are part of a larger collective network with multiple identities always at play and always being negotiated. For instance, Simone, one of the young immigrants Vieira interviews for her ethnographic work in *American by Paper*, noted a similar project as the "only college writing she described as meaningful to her," a multimodal one that "detailed the fraught process of crossing a border illegally and acquiring an education[, featuring] an image of migrants swimming across a river at night and another image of a cross in the desert for those who died in the journey" (135).

This experience gets near the sense of *avatar* that Ulmer describes and is one of the aims of the mystory genre. First, the "multimodal" project is one that acknowledges the various kinds of composition practices that electrate peoples use to make sense of their individual and collective experiences (Simone's story of crossing the border and of a memorial to those who died attempting to cross the border). Second, it demonstrates the limits of *literate* practices to fully grapple with these collective experiences while using those experiences to testify to (not argue) literacy's role as one of "passing—passing classes, passing checkpoints, passing for legal. It was about giving the right-enough information to a figure of authority with the power to deny or grant her passage" (*American* 135). As Vieira describes it, this anecdote reveals "that the punishing material realities that were tied up in her lived experiences with textuality could not be extricated from the literate site of the classroom, could not be extricated from her writing itself" (135). The thing about this description that sticks out most to me is one that resonates with Ulmer's mystory—the use of the word *passing*, in all of its various meanings across domains of knowledge. This word, for Simone and Vieira, functions as a *diegetic* term, one that, in Ulmer's words, names "that part of a narrative that persists across all media, all adaptations, translations, remakes" and gets us closer to "the kind of 'belonging together' experienced in electronic cultures" (*Internet* 5). Moreover, the mystory deviates from the literate practices of assimilation that alienate immigrant children and children of immigrants from US society by aiming to "develop rhetorical and composition practices for citizens to move from consumers to producers" of contemporary discourse practices, particularly image and other sensory-based media practices (Ulmer, *Internet* 6). As Marc Santos et al. note, "[W]hile the mystory is not the kind of direct political action sought by [James] Berlin [in his critique of expressivism], it is an important step in cultivating an agent (or, as Ulmer identifies them, an *egent*) capable of acting politically and ethically in the 21st century" (para. 6).

In brief, the aim of the mystory is to explore how the various discourse practices we engage in can be brought together in some sort of cohesive manner, represented by a guiding emblem that serves as "the founding pattern of [a person's] signature style of learning and making anything" (Ulmer, *Internet* 6). This emblem is *discovered* through memory work, by *tracing* (a term derived from Derrida's *Of Grammatology*) or mapping out the influence of networks (discourses) in order to expose how our identities are bound up with memory and material. As Santos et al. describe mystory, it "remains mindful of the material and the ways the material engenders selfhood" and "by rejuvenating our faith in personal testimony, [it] attempts to fashion a digital form of agency that returns politics back to the individual" (para. 7). Perhaps the most useful element of the mystory project, beyond returning political agency to the individual, is that it is described as an experiment that allows students to explore their own discourse practices in ways that make sense to them. By moving beyond the standard practices of literacy narratives, the mystory moves beyond the assimilating and disciplinary functions of literate writing instruction required of all students, and in the case of this chapter and collection, of immigrants. In my own case, it was this element of the mystory that led to my epiphany; it offered me an opportunity to see how my identity as an *electrate* individual allowed me to bring into conversation my immigrant status with my status as citizen. Rather than provide an argument (a literate practice), in what follows I perform a brief version of my own mystory, beginning with the documentation of an invention in my field, and followed by accounts of memories in my Family, Entertainment, and Community discourse networks. I end by presenting an emblem that evokes the look and feel of this mystory. Each section begins with assignment descriptions that Ulmer provides in *Internet Invention*.

Career Discourse: Comics and Graphic Narrative

> *Document an important discovery, or a (founding) invention, in your career domain (your university major, or a field of disciplinary knowledge in which you have some interest).* (Ulmer, *Internet* 21–22)

My scholarly interests have always gravitated toward visual and sensory media. Looking back, part of this interest stems from my early education and my family history. In first grade, our school offered classes in human-computer interaction, giving us the opportunity to play *The Oregon Trail* and *Breakout* on just-released Apple II computers. I have a difficult time separating this experience from my parents' experiences attending public schools in a rural, economically depressed farming village in north-central Portugal, each of us experiencing a new-to-our-family mode of communication. The juxtaposition of one of my first educational experiences with electronic media and my parents' experiences as the first in their families to gain access to alphabetic writing remains a particularly interesting parallel. My scholarly work has been an attempt to bridge this parallel across old, new, and emerging media, particularly through treating comics as a relay for connecting the aural and the alphabetic with the visual and the sensory—comics have minimal technology requirements (pencil and paper) and the genre was formally invented to prepare students, like my parents, to make the transition from an agrarian society to an industrial one (cf. Töpffer, *Inventing Comics*).

During my graduate work, I had only an inkling that comics could help bridge the divide between material and digital cultures, as well as literate and electrate societies, in a way that other media could not, serving as part of the reason I chose to explore in my dissertation the potential of comics as an electrate method of rhetorical invention (Figueiredo). However, only years later did I discover that there was more to this inkling; this kind of rhetorical invention was, in fact, at the heart of the medium's formalization in the nineteenth century. In 2017, I published a translation of Rodolphe Töpffer's essays (French to English) to uncover the rhetorical histories of comics and the medium's place in the field (cf. *Inventing Comics*).

Töpffer, born in 1799, was the son of two immigrants who moved from Germany to Switzerland in the late eighteenth century because Töpffer's father, Wolfgang, had secured a position as a portrait painter and caricaturist in Geneva. Töpffer's early life included training in painting and caricature alongside his father, and, in 1819, he was admitted to a university in Paris to continue the apprenticeship that began with Wolfgang. A few months into his studies (in the sister arts, including rhetoric, philosophy, literature, theater, etc.), he was diagnosed with a degenerative eye disease, returned to Geneva in 1820, and, after a brief two years working as a portrait painter, decided to pursue a teaching career. In 1822 he was hired as a teacher at a Geneva boarding school, and in 1824, with the investment by his new wife's father, started his own boarding school. His teaching focused on the classical trivium, including grammar, logic, and rhetoric. As he describes in one of his earliest published essays (see Figure 8.1), the development of comics as a pedagogical practice was marked by the emerging, modern tendency toward experimentation and invention. Specifically, he describes a new population of students, students who were not part of the ruling classes (the bourgeois or aristocracy), but students from agricultural backgrounds (the proletariat) who were enrolling in schools designed to prepare them for life in an emerging industrial era that required skilled and unskilled labor. These students, unlike the former well-to-do students, had little interest in learning Latin (a core requirement in the traditional curriculum of the time). These were students interested in learning the skills necessary to find jobs in the new economy and to support the social and cultural well-being of their families and societies. Töpffer didn't jettison this classical training, but made a conscious decision to have these students use the tools they "preferred, by which I mean pens and paper; sketching images in [their] notebooks in such a way that you would have found a beautiful Roman slaying a Cathaginian instead of a single word of proper Latin" (*Inventing Comics* 169)—comics, a method designed to bridge classical and modern approaches to education. I see my parents in Töpffer's students, and think of stories about nuns spanking them with a ruler in front of the classroom for being tardy to school, children from agricultural backgrounds being led into an emerging industrial era and the new world that would invite their labor but not their bodies or experiences.

While graphic narrative and storytelling have long histories (going back as far as the Bayeux Tapestry in the eleventh century, or even the cave paintings of the Paleolithic era),[10] Töpffer's invention of comics was not only a new method for helping a

FIGURE 8.1. *Cover of R. Töpffer's* Excursion a La Grande Chartreuse.

new population of students learn the rhetorical skills he saw as necessary for the scientific and industrial eras;[11] it was also an attempt to revive and adapt the classical practices of oral rhetorics for his own era. As Ellen Wiese puts it, Töpffer's work "seems to have intended no more than a record, fixed on paper, of the live act of oratory[, having] taken to heart the classical authorities on rhetoric, whom he met daily, of course, in his class at the Academy" (xvi). Moreover, Töpffer's essays on physiognomy and his theory-based monograph, *Essais Sur le Beau Dans Les Arts* (untranslated), foreshadows the emergence of a dramatistic approach to rhetoric,[12] describing the performative and theatrical elements of delivery. In fact, the name of the medium, *comics*, is likely a result of Töpffer's own theatrical leanings toward the comic rather than the tragic, with comedy being the mode of discourse he identifies as challenging the values presented in the morally "deleterious" novels popular in his time (*Inventing Comics* 17). The invention of comics, as a formal rhetorical exercise tied to oral communication and print-based writing practices, was conceived not only as a hybrid of image and letter, but also as a mixture of methods from the arts and humanities disciplines adapted to the technological innovations of the age (paper, printing presses, etc.). Töpffer's development of comics, to use Nick Montfort's words about Scott McCloud's work, shows "the way for contemporary thinkers who would seek to rigorously analyze emerging media" (711). Much of Töpffer's work in the nineteenth century reflects contemporary thinking about new media rhetorics and the revived role of performance in other media, such as moving image, sound, and space and place.

Briefly, comics represent the mixture of oral, literate, and electrate rhetorical practices, as well as a translingual and transmodal approach to rhetorical communication, and they point the way toward the invention of new rhetorical practices that can counter a "'monolinguistic approach to language and language relations" (Lu and Horner 213), as well as an approach to rhetorical practice more broadly (cf. Shipka). Comics challenge what Lauren Cagle, in documenting the invention of the red pen as part of her Career Discourse, calls the "metaphoric violence we do to our students when we teach them poorly and treat their writing as something to be crossed out and thoroughly corrected" (Santos et al.).[13]

Family Discourse

Document a scene that sticks in your memory from the childhood years of your family life. (Ulmer, *Internet* 86)

The most memorable moments of my childhood years took place around the kitchen table in our small home in southern New Jersey. It was where we had family dinners every night; it was where my father would listen to Benfica (his favorite *futebol* team) games on an old transistor radio he bought after being drafted into the Portuguese army. It was where my father and brother taught me to speak English in the years leading up to my enrollment in kindergarten. It was where my father tutored me in math when I struggled to make passing grades in elementary school. It was where, on my eleventh birthday, I came home to show my father how well I'd done on a math exam, thanks to his tutoring, only to find the cancer had taken its toll. And it remains the place, when I visit, where my mother and I talk late into the evening about life and the paths we've all taken since those early days. However, the memory that sticks out most takes place about ten days before my father's passing. I was on my way to a friend's house to play board games when my father pulled me aside and gave me his necklace (see Figure 8.2). He told me that this necklace was given to him by his mother on the day he left for basic training. It's a gold necklace with a crucifix and a solid sterling-silver heart pendant, which his mother said represented her own heart, the one he was taking with him as he prepared (however reluctantly) to take part in Portugal's colonial mission in Macau.

Over the years, at that same table, my mother would tell me about a conversation she and my father had when he was given the news that his cancer was terminal and that he had only weeks left. His biggest regret was that he wouldn't be able to see his children graduate from high school and enroll in college. Both my father and mother wanted their children to surpass them in education, gainful employment, and wisdom. They saw their children as part of an "ongoing narrative" that they projected "into our care ... as sons" (Ulmer, *Internet* 86). Education, for my parents, like the Brazilian immigrants Vieira describes in *American by Paper*,

From Orality to Electracy: A Mystory

FIGURE 8.2. *My father's necklace.*

was linked "not with assimilation but with mobility, pervading their motivations for moving and their plans for the future" (29), "not in the service of national ideals, but instead to achieve social and economic success for themselves and their families" (54). The goal for my parents, as with so many other Portuguese immigrants in our local communities, was and remains encapsulated in the phrase *ir para frente*—keep moving forward "the stories of [our] lives" and our family histories (112).

The kitchen table was also the place where my mother would tell me the story of our family's immigration to the United States. In my mother's teenage years, she put to work her family's new access to literacy when she wrote to an uncle living in New Jersey, asking if it would be possible for him to bring her to the United States. Her uncle responded that he wouldn't be able to bring her over but could find a way to secure a green card for her father (my grandfather) as a part of a work program. My grandfather didn't want to leave his family again, having spent the first decade of his marriage to my grandmother working in Brazil so that my grandmother could buy parcels of land and build the family farm. However, at the urging of my grandmother, he took the opportunity and eventually secured his entire family's legal passage to the States. It is not lost on my mother that only four years of schooling gave her access to writing and made this passage to the United States possible. Years later, after my father had completed his required military service, he reunited with his sister and her husband, who had immigrated to France for the same reasons my mother's family immigrated to the United States—social and financial mobility. Using his own access to literacy, he began corresponding with my mother via "the post," and eventually

FIGURE 8.3. *The gate to my grandmother's farm (left) and my father's childhood home (right).*

proposed marriage in a love letter. They started their new life together in southern New Jersey and bought the home where the kitchen table still stands, reminders of times gone by.

On family trips to Portugal, we would stay at my grandmother's farm, which is catty-corner to the home where my father was born and raised. I think about how my father's mother presented the necklace to him (see Figure 8.3). The space between my mother's and my father's childhood homes is a site of mediation and theoretical invention that Ulmer calls *chora*—the practice of adding "an identification with a specific location to the mystorical identification with a protagonist in each of the popcycle institutions" (*Internet* 101). In this space, I feel what the Portuguese call a sense of *saudades*, a temperament that expresses a deep emotional state of nostalgia or profound melancholic longing (cf. Emmons and Lewis 402). I will never know what it was like to grow up in this place and in this (oral) society. And yet I return to this place when I think of my family's journey to the United States, and of the desires that my mother and father had for their children—to keep moving forward while acknowledging that we are characters in the ongoing narrative of the family. The necklace my father passed down to me is a reminder of where this narrative began—a small farming village in Portugal, where, like my mother and father, I used to play *futebol* in the streets with distant cousins.

Entertainment Discourse

> *Document the details of a movie or TV narrative some part of which you still remember from your childhood years (K–12).* (Ulmer, *Internet* 127)

In place of a movie or TV narrative, I want to focus on a book. For Ulmer the artifact in this section matters less than connecting family memories to the entertainment narrative, and to exploring "the hero's quest" as an expression of "an ancient ritual of initiation—the achievement of individual identity" (*Internet Invention* 126). In my case, the book is Antoine de Saint-Exupéry's *The Little Prince*.[14] The narrative is a fairly straightforward work of imagination. A prince lives on and oversees a small planet with a flower he adores and cares for. Feeling lonely one day, the little prince decides to travel to other planets to explore other worlds and the kinds of people who live on them. Before arriving on Earth, the prince has visited six other planets, inhabited by a king with no subjects, a man who thinks of himself as the most admirable individual on his planet (no one else lives there), a drunk, a businessman who spends his days counting the stars without acknowledging their beauty, a lamplighter who wastes his life lighting and putting out lamps every sixty seconds, and a geographer, respectively. Each figure is meant to represent the problems of specialization—a person who works tirelessly at one thing and ignores all other fields, family, and friends.

My first exposure to this book was during my junior year of high school, when I read it in the original French as part of a foreign language class unit. I had enrolled in French classes every year of high school to learn the language my father's sister, her husband, and their children spoke and wrote. While I want to think of my role in my Family Discourse as analogous to the hero's quest of the little prince, I feel much more like the narrator. I think of the little prince as a sage to whom I have returned over the years for guidance when faced with major life changes. The scene that resonates most with me is the one when the little prince first meets the narrator and asks the narrator to draw him a sheep. Upon considering the request, the narrator responds that he doesn't know how to draw. The prince, not letting up, retorts, "That doesn't matter. Draw me a sheep . . ." (8). By this point in the narrative, the narrator has already recounted his attempts, as a child, to draw a boa constrictor from the inside and from the outside, and the less-than-supportive responses to the drawing from grownups. And as he thinks about how to respond to the prince, he remembers that his education has focused on "geography, history, arithmetic, and grammar" (8).

Upon revisiting the narrative, the associations between my career and family discourses are obvious. The little prince's insistence that the narrator draw a sheep despite not knowing how to draw directly parallels the theory Töpffer develops in his writings about comics, including the prince's distaste for specialized discourse practices and his dislike of "the tone of a moralist" (23). While I had not addressed it in my Family Discourse, my experiences parallel those of the narrator—critiques of my drawings in early childhood. At the urging of my parents and the tutoring of my father, I slowly left drawing behind in order to pursue more academic goals, starting my academic life as a computer science major.

The position of the narrator in his diegetic world is analogous to my position in my family; this narrative "figures the atmosphere or mood of the family situation," formed "around problems" and conflict (Ulmer, *Internet* 127). The mood of the narrative is similar to the feeling I get standing in the street between my mother's and my father's childhood homes: *saudades*. The little prince reflects this sense of longing for something ontologically human that's been lost in highly specialized societies, saying, "[W]hat is essential is invisible to the eye" (87), a state of mind a child brings to the world. As the switchman the little prince meets late in the story tells us, "Only children are flattening their noses against the windowpanes. Only the children know what they are looking for. They waste their time over a rag doll and it becomes very important to them" (89). The lesson we learn from the little prince is to foster this kind of childlike curiosity and playful experimentation within ourselves and our communities.

The "rag doll" functions as a relay for Saint-Exupéry's narrator in the same way my father's necklace functions as a relay for me, not as a token or a fetish object, but an object that returns me to the street between my parents' childhood homes and to the kitchen table in my childhood home. It reflects the time "wasted" learning the discourse of specialization and standardization required by literate institutions. The prince teaches us that there is no wasted time when telling stories about our family histories and how those stories have come to inform the kind of social and rhetorical practices we value. Drawing without knowing how to draw is a practice of rhetorical invention, a way of moving forward while acknowledging the histories that have led each of us to a given kairotic moment in our lives, in the same way that letters, like the one my mother wrote to her uncle, serve "as an antidote to the *saudade*, the missing or nostalgia, caused by separation" (Vieira, *American* 60). As Vieira notes, "[L]etters were part of an earlier media-scape" that "entered into homes, projecting life and people elsewhere in a particularly inviting way" (64); drawing (which also reflects composing in another form) is part of the industrial and postindustrial media-scape through which we keep moving forward.

Community Discourse

> *Document an exemplary story from your community, that is a story about a person or event that your community identifies with and tells about itself in its celebrations, festivals, naming practices (of streets, buildings, parks), memorials.* (Ulmer, *Internet* 191–92)

The Community portion of mystory is directly connected to the Entertainment section, specifically in the way the "hero's quest" serves as a relay for thinking "the relationship among all the actants" (Ulmer, *Internet* 186). The community represents a "value" or value system "coming from the community as Sender," the purpose of which is to identify "what the community thinks for us, and prior to us on our behalf" (191–92). While this portion tends to focus on hometowns, Ulmer also suggests that "it is possible to define 'community' not as a nation but in terms of religion, race, or ethnicity, when the collective stories that one grew up with took precedence over the story of the nation and state told in public schools" (192). In my case, all of these terms merged and led me to choose a community separate from each: the punk community.

My hometown was and is marked by a few communities. The ones that resonate most with me are the Portuguese immigrant and Brazilian immigrant communities, as well as the dominant local community that showed animosity toward both.[15] While I had my own run-ins with locals, often being called a "pork chop"[16] in elementary and middle school, I didn't feel comfortable positioning myself in the local Portuguese community, which had brought to the United States a common element of agrarian life (one that I resisted). "It takes a village to raise a child" was more than a saying, it was a practice, and one I didn't feel comfortable with because of the ideology of surveillance it represented.

This state of mind, resisting the surveillance apparatus, was a key marker in my relationship to these communities and the values that those communities tried to impose on me, and it's one that built the grounding for my association with the punk community. The punk community embodied what I saw as my own general state of mind, a feeling that I belonged neither in the community of my school-age peers or in my ethnic community. It embodies the sense of resistance to "growing up" that the little prince imparts to the narrator, the resistance to the ethos of authority and expertise. It embodies the kinds of rhetorical practices Töpffer proposes for those drawing comics, an amateur art that satirizes and confronts the ideology of expertise through the invention of new cultural practices in a moment of insight (aha!). I had adopted a desire for learning and the *ir para frente* state of mind my mother and father emphasized at home.

The state of mind bringing all of these values together is one that Dick Hebdige calls the *intellectual punk,* defined by punk's determination to detach "from the taken-for-granted landscape of normalized forms" (19) and its "'unnatural' synthesis" of "diverse and superficially incompatible" traditions (26–27). There's a sense of invention to punk that embodies attempts to synthesize parts of everyday life that get lost in official/authoritative histories of communities, which Sirc has explicated beautifully in *English Composition as a Happening*. As Sirc writes, the ideological position of mastery/specialization/expertise orders "texts and selves and worlds" (238); punk counters this ideology by caring "only about the unforeseen possibilities of writing, the process, and play" (241). Perhaps more than anything, it was this sensibility that led to my interest in the literary, artistic, and rhetorical vanguard, the performative, experimental, and theoretical movements that push our field beyond literate understandings of language and media practices. As I learned from my grandparents, both language and media are experienced as *happenings* or *events* in a particular, embodied, and performative experience. To standardize them feels unnatural.

Emblem

Design an emblem that evokes the look and feel of your mystory. (Ulmer, *Internet* 246–47)

The image in Figure 8.4 is taken from my Career Discourse—an image from one of Töpffer's nineteenth-century travel sketchbooks, composed during one of several summer field trips he guided his students on as they explored the European countryside as the Industrial Revolution was remaking those landscapes. The quote (motto) comes from Friedrich Nietzsche's *The Gay Science* (or, *The Joyful Wisdom*). In the image, Töpffer draws a student sporting a backpack and running toward the horizon (and/or away from the expert artist/author/scholar/teacher) against a simply drawn landscape. The mood of this image ties together the documentation in each of my popcycle discourses, reflecting the sense of "moving forward" (*ir para frente*) found in my family discourse; the kind of drawing practices that the little prince challenges the narrator of *The Little Prince* to adopt in my entertainment discourse; and the punk sensibilities of going one's own way, resisting surveillance (we can't see the character's face), and performative, experimental play found in my community

FIGURE 8.4. *Emblem (image of the wide scope)*.

discourse. From my Career Discourse, the image also evokes a translingual and transmodal approach to composition practices and the way that communication practices are treated as ways of negotiating meaning across "different modes, genres, materials, cultural practices, communicative technologies, and language varieties" (Shipka 251). The quote from Nietzsche bridges these various discourses by synthesizing the states of mind found in each discourse—of moving forward (in one's chosen path), of play and experimentation with communication practices, and of resisting social, cultural, and political attempts to assimilate these disparate domains of experience.

Conclusion

The mystory project is not designed specifically to support first-generation immigrants and children of immigrants in exploring the ways in which their various identities form and evolve, nor is it designed to offer a solution to the problems faced by those individuals who are navigating language, media, and cultural meaning, or to critique systems of oppression. Rather, the mystory is a project that allows individuals to explore how identities are formed and to invent their identities anew, in the tradition of humanistic inquiry. As Ulmer explains, "[I]dentity, both individual and collective, is an imagined identity, mediated and sustained by a consistent and continuously updated narrative. The identity of an individual, a nation, an empire, a civilization, may be altered by altering the story it tells about itself" (*Internet* 320). The motivations that have led me to a career as a teacher-scholar of writing, rhetoric, and media are grounded in multiple, overlapping stories I have told about myself. Much like my grandparents, these stories evolve as (particular) events demand.[17] As Marc Santos and colleagues note, the "purpose and power of Ulmer's postpedagogical project is to invest students in the possibility of inventing new, localized, contingent, and multiple answers," to expose "the ambivalence between the personal and academic," and to give students an opportunity to use their backgrounds as a way of finding their space/place in cultural and disciplinary domains, as well as avoiding the trap of attempting to discover some "underlying authentic individual" self. The stories the mystory prompts a student to explicate and mediate "use . . . individual experiences and memories as a lens for understanding cultural dynamics and inventing new forms of expression."

By way of conclusion, I want to return to Kate Vieira's work. She writes that the literacy lives of young immigrants call on us to develop approaches to rhetorical communication practices that "address young writers' and readers' larger social worlds in ways that can be both pedagogically productive and humanizing for marginalized groups" and that work against "the literacy pressures bearing down on transnational young adults" (*American* 112). For these young adults, "literacy accrued meaning as it circulated, socially and materially, across . . . various nodes" (140). More to the point, Vieira points out the problems with maintaining the research focus on literacy: from the perspective of the immigrants who "shared their lives with" Vieira,

> the meaning of literacy often departs from what scholars and others have previously thought. If literacy has been theorized

as a social *practice,* the people in this study also experienced literacy as its sociomaterial *product.* If literacy has been connected to *identity,* many also viewed literacy in relation to written *identification.* If literacy has been linked to its *social context,* many also saw literacy as a technology of *decontextualization.* If literacy educators have hoped that literacy *empowers* and *humanizes,* for many migrants literacy also *oppressed* and *alienated.* If policy makers have touted literacy a way [sic] to *assimilate,* many migrants hoped to use it to *move.* The stories people shared with me . . . ask scholars, educators, and policy makers to consider the conditions under which literacy may also be experienced quite differently, expanding our theories of what literacy is and does. (*American* 146)

My hope is that, through this performance of the mystory project, I have contributed to the ongoing invention of practices that can help us and our students address these conditions. Like the second-generation Azorean American immigrant Vieira quotes, my parents also came to the United States for a better life; "[t]hey only had a fourth-grade education . . . but they had intelligence" (*American* 159), and they wanted their children to *ir para frente.* While they may have focused this phrase on education and social mobility, it has come to mean something more—to keep moving our family forward in ways that stich together the familiar stories of Portuguese immigrants and our own particular experiences as immigrants. The mystory project has helped to facilitate this understanding of the ongoing narrative and forward movement central to those experiences.

Notes

1. As Vieira writes, "[Y]oung people in this study showed little concern with English or assimilation. Their most significant experiences of literacy were more material than linguistic, more transnational than assimilative, more pragmatic than ideological. English could be learned" (*American* 139).

2. http://sophist.people.clemson.edu/801.html. Accessed 3 Mar. 2019.

3. http://sophist.people.clemson.edu/802.html. Accessed 3 Mar. 2019.

4. This comment is specifically focused on what Brian Street calls the "autonomous" model of literacy, which exists independently of the actions and ideologies of the people engaging in such work, including how it is "constructed for a specific political purpose" (19)—the desire for acculturation (assimilation) to the culture-specific practices and the ideologies of "individual liberty and social mobility" (1–2) encompassed in the idea of the American Dream.

5. Literacy, as Vieira has pointed out, "held the promise of mobility" ("Literacy Studies" 515), which my parents leveraged to move outside the confines of their parents' farming village.

6. See Geoff Sirc's *English Composition as a Happening*.

7. For another take on how this genre has been used to explore the roles of technologies, institutions, and selfhood, see Santos and colleagues' webtext, "Our [Electrate] Stories: Explicating Ulmer's Mystory Genre." As they write, "In terms of selfhood, Ulmer offered *avatar*, a term borrowed from video gaming, as a replacement for the literate concept of subjectivity and the oral concept of spirit. An avatar's agency is contingent upon its place within a network: like a player in a game, it is neither powerless nor autonomous. An avatar is always at work within a larger system yet retains the ability to change the system." As such, the mystory aligns well with Shipka's call for attending to the range of conventions we and our students engage with in any communication act.

8. For more on the connection between multimodality, translanguaging, and rhetorical genres, see Laura Gonzales's article "Multimodality, Translangualism, and Rhetorical Genre Studies."

9. See Ulmer, *Avatar Emergency*.

10. See Thomas Rickert's essay, "Rhetorical Prehistory and the Paleolithic."

11. Much of Töpffer's work is aimed at critiquing mechanical reproduction and the pseudosciences of physiognomy and phrenology.

12. See Kenneth Burke's *A Grammar of Motives*.

13. See Laura Gonzales for an examination of how such practices can challenge the kind of "violence" Cagle describes. As Gonzales writes, "By highlighting students' experiences with multimodality, and by moving away from the linear, container-bound approach to writing, we might continue unbinding genres from rigid forms, languages, and classrooms, seeing and teaching them as ways of meaning-making across contexts.

These ways of making meaning will continue to expand as languages and technologies keep shifting and as the field of rhetorical genre studies continues to account for and partake in these changes" (para. 65). Coincidentally, the example assignment Gonzales uses for this study is based in the practice of comics composition—drawing.

14. Unfortunately, due to copyright laws, I am unable to include any images from this book in this essay.

15. Members of the Portuguese and Brazilian communities also had their own animosity toward each other, with the Portuguese members seeing Brazilians as having cheated the immigration system. In fact, as I was reading Vieira's ethnography comparing Azorean, Azorean Americans, and Brazilians in South Mills, Massachusetts, it felt like reading about my own hometown, hearing the critiques of Brazilian Portuguese that were only emphasized by the privileged "legal status [that] reinforced" the Portuguese immigrants (Vieira, *American* 47).

16. A derogatory ethnic epithet used to describe Portuguese people, most often indicating a characteristic of being overweight; obesity. (Side note: I was not overweight as a child.)

17. In the Deleuzian sense of the term. See *The Logic of Sense*.

Works Cited

Anzaldúa, Gloria. *Borderlands/La Frontera: The New Mestiza*. Aunt Lute Books, 1987.

Arroyo, Sarah J. "Growing Up with Electracy." *Enculturation: A Journal of Rhetoric, Writing, and Culture*, 22 Nov. 2016, http://encultura tion.net/growing-up-with-electracy. Accessed 2 Mar. 2018.

——— . *Participatory Composition: Video Culture, Writing, and Electracy*. Southern Illinois UP, 2013.

Bartholomae, David. *Writing on the Margins: Essays on Composition and Teaching*. Bedford/St. Martin's, 2005.

Burke, Kenneth. *A Grammar of Motives*. Forgotten Books, 2018.

Deleuze, Gilles. *The Logic of Sense*. Edited by Constantin V. Boundas, translated by Mark Lester with Charles Stivale, Columbia UP, 1993.

Emmons, Shirlee, and Wilbur Watkin Lewis. *Researching the Song: A Lexicon.* Oxford UP, 2006.

Figueiredo, Sergio, "Un/Composing (Visual) Rhetorics: A (Strange) Comic(s) View of Writing in the Age of New Media." Clemson University, 2011. *All Dissertations,* 705, https://tigerprints.clemson.edu/all_dissertations/705.

Gonzales, Laura. "Multimodality, Translingualism, and Rhetorical Genre Studies." *Composition Forum,* vol. 31, Spring 2015, http://compositionforum.com/issue/31/multimodality.php.

Guerra, Juan C. "Cultivating a Rhetorical Sensibility in the Translingual Writing Classroom." *College English,* vol. 78, no. 3, 2016, pp. 228–33.

Havelock, Eric. *The Muse Learns to Write: Reflections on Orality and Literacy from Antiquity to the Present.* Yale UP, 1986.

Hebdige, Dick. *Subculture: The Meaning of Style.* Routledge, 1979.

Lu, Min-Zhan, and Bruce Horner. "Introduction: Translingual Work." *College English,* vol. 78, no. 3, 2016, pp. 207–18.

Montfort, Nick. "Introduction: Time Frames." *The New Media Reader,* edited by Noah Wardrip-Fruin and Nick Montfort, MIT P, 2003.

Nietzsche, Friedrich Wilhelm. *The Gay Science: With a Prelude in Rhymes and an Appendix of Songs.* Translated by Walter Kaufmann, Vintage, 1974.

Ong, Walter J. *Orality & Literacy: The Technologizing of the Word.* Routledge, 1982.

———. "Writing Is a Technology That Restructures Thought." *The Written Word: Literacy in Transition,* edited by Gerd Baumann, Oxford UP, 1986, pp. 23–50.

Rickert, Thomas. "'Hands Up, You're Free': Composition in a Post-Oedipal World." *JAC: A Journal of Composition Theory,* vol. 21, no. 2, 2001, pp. 287–320.

———. "Rhetorical Prehistory and the Paleolithic." *Review of Communication,* vol. 16, no. 4, 2016, pp. 352–73.

Saint-Exupéry, Antoine de. *The Little Prince.* Harcourt Brace Jovanovich, 1971.

Santos, Marc C., Ella R. Bieze, Lauren E. Cagle, Jason Carabelli, Zachary P. Dixon, Kristen N. Gay, Sarah Beth Hopton, and Megan M. McIntyre. "Our [Electrate] Stories: Explicating Ulmer's Mystory Genre." *Kairos: A Journal of Rhetoric, Technology, and Pedagogy*, vol. 18, no. 2, 2014, http://kairos.technorhetoric.net/18.2/praxis/santos-et-al/index.html.

Shipka, Jody. "Transmodality in/and Processes of Making: Changing Dispositions and Practice." *College English*, vol. 78, no. 3, 2016, pp. 250–57.

Sirc, Geoffrey. *English Composition as a Happening*. Utah State UP, 2002.

Street, Brian V. *Literacy in Theory and Practice*. Cambridge UP, 1984.

Töpffer, Rodolphe. *Inventing Comics: A New Translation of Rodolphe Töpffer's Reflections on Graphic Storytelling, Media Rhetorics, & Aesthetic Practice*. Translated by Sergio C. Figueiredo, Parlor Press, 2017.

Ulmer, Gregory L. *Avatar Emergency*. Parlor Press, 2012.

———. *Heuretics: The Logic of Invention*. Johns Hopkins UP, 1994.

———. *Internet Invention: From Literacy to Electracy*. Longman, 2003.

Vieira, Kate. *American by Paper: How Documents Matter in Immigrant Literacy*. U of Minnesota P, 2016.

———. "Literacy Studies in the 1990s: Moving through Space, Moving with Time." *College Composition and Communication*, vol. 69, no. 3, 2018, pp. 510–19.

———. "On the Social Consequences of Literacy." *Literacy in Composition Studies*, vol. 1, no. 1, 2013, pp. 26–32.

Villanueva, Victor, Jr. *Bootstraps: From an American Academic of Color*. National Council of Teachers of English, 1993.

Wiese, Ellen. "Introduction: Rudolphe Töpffer and the Language of Physiognomy." *Enter: the Comics: Rudolphe Töpffer's Essay on Physiognomy and the True Story of Monsieur Crepin*. U of Nebraska P, 1965.

Index

Accented English. *See* English language, accented
Adichi, Chimamanda Ngozi, 58
Adjunct teachers, 34–35
Ahmed, Sara, 3–4
Alexander, Kara Poe, 9
Althusser, Louis, 156–57n5
Alvarez, Julia, 47
Alvarez, Steven, 49, 63, 105, 113, 115
Anzaldúa, Gloria, 111, 146–47, 155
Arroyo, Sarah, 161
Assimilation, 30
Avatars, 164, 181n7

Balester, Valerie M., 52
Bartholomae, David, 160
Bhabha, Homi, 87, 90
Bhattacharya, Piyali, 70
Bilingual Education Act, 106–7
Bilingual individuals. *See* Multilingual classrooms; Nonnative English speakers (NNES)
Bollywood movies, 60
Border pedagogy, 97
Bourdieu, Pierre, 7–8, 45, 82, 126, 130–31
Brandt, Deborah, 62
Bratta, Phil, 3
Broken English. *See* English language, accented
Brown, M. Christopher II, 90

Cagle, Lauren, 169

Callahan, Sara B. Dykins, 131
Care, ethic of. *See* Ethic of care
Chandler, Erin T., 73
Cisneros, Sandra, 29
Citizenship, 110, 157n7
Clance, Pauline Rose, 113, 114
Cobos, Casie, 3, 5
Code switching, 65, 108, 109–10, 146–47, 152, 157n6
Comics, 166–69
Community, 175–77
Comparative rhetoric, 2
Counterstories, 6, 8, 9–10, 104. *See also* Literacy
Cox, Michelle, 33
Critical race theory (CRT), 45
CRT. *See* Critical race theory (CRT)
Cultural capital, 7, 45, 130
Cultural literacy. *See* Discourse, American

Dancy, T. Elon II, 90
Daniel, Thompson, Jay, 90
Dayton, Amy, 73
Deidentification, 91, 113
Delgado, Richard, 18
De los Reyes, Chloe, 6, 18–28
Difference-as-relation, 96–97
Discourse, American. *See also* Identity; Otherness
 defined, 24–25
 and identity, 65–66
 as "identity kit," 39n8
 and pop culture, 59–61
Dunbar, Paul Laurence, 65

INDEX

Economic capital, 130
Edbauer, Jenny, 92
Education
  and feminism, 71
  and social mobility, 46, 58, 67, 73–74, 171
Educational system
  as difficult to navigate, for nonnative English speakers (NNES), 27–29
  supports for navigating, 62–63
Electracy
  defined, 148, 150–51
  and mystory genre, 163–64
Emblem, 177–78
English language, accented. *See also* Literacy
  and citizenship, 110
  and code switching, 109
  and "deficiency" label of nonnative English Speakers (NNES), 24–26
  institutional prejudice against, 88–89
  as liability, in institutional language policy, 128
  as marker of Otherness, 26, 50
English Only movement, 127
Ethic of care, 2, 12n1
Ethnography, 54, 96
Ethos, 110–13, 116–17

Falcón, Jennifer, 7, 45–49, 52–53
Family separation policy, xii–xiii
Fay, Elizabeth A., 69
Feminism, 71
Figueiredo, Sergio, 8–9
First-generation students/academics. *See also* specific academics
  cultural expectations for, 70–72
  educational support programs for, 51
  education viewed as key to social mobility for, 46, 58, 67, 73–74
  and imposter syndrome, 7, 72, 89–90
  and institutional confirmation of English literacy, 88–89
  language brokering performed by, 63–64, 75
  liminal spaces inhabited by, 90
  motives for entering rhetoric and composition field, 31–32, 51, 144–45
  and Otherness, 69
  and social class, 69–70
  and success/deficiency conflict, 17–18
  use of term, 102n
Fox, Steve, 129
Fry, Richard, 43

Ganti, Tejaswini, 60
Garcia, Ofelia, 106–7, 109, 117
Gardner, Susan K., 69, 71
Gee, James Paul, 23, 39n8
Gender issues, 70–72
Gilyard, Keith, 134, 135
Giroux, Henry, 97
Gonzales, Laura, 109, 117, 181–82n13
Goodall, Harold Lloyd Jr., 125
Grosik, Sarah Arva, 28
Guerra, Juan, 12, 92, 162
Guglielmo, Letizia, 6, 8

Hamilton, Sharon Jean, 72
Harklau, Linda, 26
Harris, Joseph, 32
Hebdige, Dick, 176
Hechinger, Fred M., 128
Herrmann, Rachel, 90
Hoggart, Richard, 31
Holley, Karri A., 71
hooks, bell, 93
Horner, Bruce, 36, 97, 117, 169
Hybridity, 90, 92–93, 115–16, 139, 145–46, 148, 151, 155

Index

Identity
  and American Discourse, 39n8, 65–66
  balancing of, for nonnative English speakers (NNES), 25, 30
  "borderland," 147
  and code switching, 152
  and deidentification, 91
  fluidity of, 134
  hybridity of, 145–46, 148, 151, 155
  and labels, 36–37
  and motionality, 92–93
  and naming, 87–88
  and school settings, 11
  Ulmer on, 179
  work of, 135–36
  Yang on, 30–31
Imes, Suzanne, 113, 114
Immigrant bargain, 105, 114
Immigrants. *See* Nonnative English speakers (NNES)
Immigration
  de los Reyes's experience of, 18–22
  Guglielmo's experience of, 104–8
  of Kumari's parents, 57–59
  Palacio's experience of, 140–42
Imposter syndrome, 7, 72, 89–90, 113–15
Institutional language policy
  accented English as liability in, 128, 132
  conflation of English language primacy and teaching effectiveness in, 124, 127
  effect of, 129
  function of, 128
  multilingualism as liability in, 126
  overview of, 123–24
  as repressive, 135
Intellectual punk, 176

Interdependence-in-difference, 134
Interface, 3

Jarratt, Susan C., 90–92
Jones, Rebecca, 111–12

Kanno, Yasuko, 28
Kells, Michelle Hall, 52
Kennedy, George, 2
Kerschbaum, Stephanie L., 96
Kim, Soo Hyon, 36
Kovalyova, Natalia, 8
Kumari, Ashanka, 7, 59–60, 112
Kynard, Carmen, 8
  on inequity in rhetoric and composition field, 37–38
  on literacy and class, 105, 112
  on multiplicity of classroom languages, 1
  on racism in academic settings, 34
  on social justice and literacy, 116

Labels
  of "deficiency," applied to nonnative English speakers (NNES), 22–26, 32–33, 35–36, 48, 106–7
  and identity, 36–37
  multitude of, applied to first-generation academics, 32
  as necessary traps, 36–37
  power of, 38
Language brokering
  Alvarez on, 63
  defined, 49–50
  as empowerment strategy, 54
  performed by first-generation students, 63–64, 75
Latinx students
  demographics of, at UTEP, 43–44
  and university diversity initiatives, 47–48

INDEX

Leonard, Rebecca Lorimer, 117
Liminal spaces, 90, 131, 147–48
Linguistic capital, 130–31
Literacy. *See also* Counterstories
  autonomous model of, 181n4
  defined, 149–50
  as empowering, xii, xiii, 171–72
  fluidity of, 109–12
  function of, 117
  and power, 103–4
  repressive uses of, xi–xii, 10, 135, 159–61
  and social class, 105, 112–13, 181n5
  Vieira on, 179–80, 180n1
The Little Prince (Saint-Exupéry), 173–75
Lovejoy, Kim Brian, 129
Lu, Min-Zhan, 97, 169

Mao, LuMing, 134
Martinez, Aja, 6, 18, 104
Massumi, Brian, 5
Matsuda, Paul Kei, 118
Maulucci, Mária S. Rivera, 86–87
Mayshle, Peter, 7–8
Memmi, Albert, 33–34
Méndez-Newman, Beatrice, 54–55
Mensah, Felicia Moore, 86–87
Migration, 156n1
Minh-ha, Trinh T., 90–92
Montfort, Nick, 169
Moss, Beverly J., 65–66
Motionality, 92–93
Multilingual classrooms, 52–54
Myers, Nancy, 111–12
Mystory genre
  aim of, 179
  avatars, 164
  career discourse, 166–69
  community discourse, 175–77
  emblem, 177–78
  entertainment discourse, 173–75
  family discourse, 170–73
  overview of, 163–66

Names
  Bourdieu on, 82
  Mayshle's experience of, 82–86
  and Otherness, 79–80
  questioning of, as Othering, 83–84, 86
Naming
  and identity, 11, 87–88
  as political act, 86–87
  and writing, 93–98
Nietzsche, Friedrich, 177–78
9/11, 66, 160
NNES. *See* Nonnative English speakers (NNES)
Nonnative English speakers (NNES)
  "deficiency" label applied to, 22–26, 32–33, 35–36, 48, 106–7
  education system as difficult to navigate for, 27–29, 62–63
  "fresh off the boat," 24
  and identity, 25, 30
  and language brokering, 49–50
North Face jacket, 68–70
Nosowitz, Dan, 108
Nursing field, 20, 21, 27–28
Nye, Naomi Shihab, 27, 95

Ohio State University (OSU), 46–48
Ong, Walter J., 150, 161–62
Orality, 146, 149
Ortmeier-Hooper, Christina, 24
OSU. *See* Ohio State University (OSU)
Otherness
  accented English as marker of, 26, 50
  and names, 79–80, 83–84, 86

Index

and performance of "Americanness," 65–66, 68–69, 112–13

Palacio, Estefany, 8, 131
Papers, 157n7
Pedagogical practices
  border pedagogy, 97
  in multilingual classrooms, 52–54
  writing to name, 93–98
Philippines, de los Reyes's experience of, 18–21
Pop culture, 59–61
Powell, Malea, 3
Punk community, 176–77

Racism, 10, 26. *See also* Xenophobia
Ratcliffe, Krista, 111, 116
Reynolds, Nedra, 111, 116
Rhetoric and composition studies
  first-generation academics' motives for entering, 31–32, 51, 74, 144–45
  Kynard on inequity in, 37–38
  racism in, 34
  at UTEP, 44
Rice, Jeff, 156n1
Rickert, Thomas, 160
Rodriguez, Richard, 31, 32
Ryan, Kathleen J., 111–12

Saint-Exupéry, Antoine de, 173–75
Santos, Marc C., 163, 164, 165, 169, 179, 181n7
Shipka, Jody, 162–63, 178, 181n7
Sirc, Geoff, 160, 177
Smith, Robert Courtney, 105
Social class
  and literacy, 105, 112–13, 181n5
  tensions of, for first-generation academics, 69–70

Social mobility
  education viewed as key to, 46, 58, 67, 73–74, 171
  and immigrant bargain, 105
Spivak, Gayatri Chakravorty, 90–91
Stewart, Kathleen, 4
Street, Brian, 181n4
Symbolic capital, 130

Tan, Amy, 25, 28, 73–74
Taylor, Paul, 43
Technology, 142–43, 151–54
Tinoco, Lizbett, 7, 49–51, 53–54
Tokarczyk, Michelle M., 69
Töpffer, Rodolphe, 167–69, 174, 176, 177–78
Translingualism, 92–93, 117, 134–35, 162
Transmodality, 162

UCLA. *See* University of California, Los Angeles (UCLA)
Ulmer, Gregory, 9, 148, 150, 161
  on avatars, 164, 181n7
  on community, 176
  on identity, 179
  on mystory, 164
University of California, Los Angeles (UCLA), 50–51
University of Texas at El Paso (UTEP), 43–44
UTEP. *See* University of Texas at El Paso (UTEP)

Vieira, Kate, 117, 159, 164–65, 175, 179, 180n1, 182n15
Villanueva, Victor, 26, 30, 37, 52
Vitanza, Victor, 161

Wan, Amy J., xi–xii
Wiese, Ellen, 169
Williams, Raymond, 88

Wills, Katherine V., 129
Wolf, Margery, 96

Xenophobia, 10, 26. *See also* Institutional language policy; Racism

Yang, Jun, 30–31
Yergeau, Melanie, 104
Yosso, Tara J., 45
Young, Morris, 110, 112, 116–17

Zheng, Xuan, 33

EDITORS

Sergio C. Figueiredo is associate professor of English, specializing in professional writing, rhetoric, and media, at Kennesaw State University. He is the translator of *Inventing Comics: A New Translation of Rodolphe Töpffer's Reflections on Graphic Storytelling, Media Rhetorics, and Aesthetic Practice*.

Letizia Guglielmo is professor of English and interdisciplinary studies and coordinator of the Gender and Women's Studies Program at Kennesaw State University. Her research and writing focus on feminist rhetoric and pedagogy, gender and pop culture, the intersections of feminist action and digital communication, and professional development for students and faculty. She is editor of *MTV and Teen Pregnancy: Critical Essays on* 16 and Pregnant *and* Teen Mom (2013), coauthor of *Scholarly Publication in a Changing Academic Landscape: Models for Success* (2014), coeditor of *Contingent Faculty Publishing in Community: Case Studies for Successful Collaborations* (2015), and editor of *Misogyny in American Culture: Causes, Trends, and Solutions* (2018).

Contributors

Chloe de los Reyes holds an MA in English from California State University, San Bernardino and has continued to teach in several departments at the same institution: in the English department's First-Year Writing Program, the International Extension Programs, and the Educational Opportunity Program. She also recently began teaching part-time at Crafton Hills College. Her scholarly interests include writing center studies; collaboration; multilingual writing; the intersections of applied linguistics and composition studies; the intersections of language, identity, and culture; and adjunct advocacy. She has presented at various conferences both nationally and internationally. She coauthored a chapter entitled "Being a Linguistic Foreigner: Learning from International Tutoring" in the second edition of *ESL Writers: A Guide for Writing Center Tutors* and also coauthored a piece on adjunct status in a forthcoming issue of *Forum: Issues about Part-Time and Contingent Faculty*.

Jennifer Falcón earned both her PhD, in rhetoric and composition, and her MFA, in creative writing, from the University of Texas at El Paso (UTEP), and her BA in English from The Ohio State University. Before joining the University of California, San Diego's Analytical Writing Program, she taught Rhetoric and Composition I and II, Workplace Writing, and Technical Communication in the undergraduate Rhetoric and Writing Studies Program at UTEP. Her research focuses on digital literacy, specifically how theories and practices in digital rhetoric, electracy, and procedural rhetoric, when applied, can enhance multimodal composition assignments in a first-year writing curriculum.

Natalia Kovalyova holds a doctorate in communication studies from the University of Texas at Austin, an MEd in international education from the University of Massachusetts at Amherst, and an MA in American studies from University College Dublin. Her research lies at the intersections of discourse, power, and persuasion in a variety of contexts, from presidential communication to media reporting to academic writing. Her recent research focuses on emergent public forums, political rationalities, and the rise of authoritarianism.

CONTRIBUTORS

Ashanka Kumari is an assistant professor of English, composition, and rhetoric at Texas A&M University, Commerce. Her research interests include graduate student professionalization, multimodal composition and pedagogy, and the intersections between identity studies, digital literacies, social media, and popular culture. Her recent dissertation, *Remaking Identities, Reworking Graduate Study: Stories from First-Generation-to-College PhD Students on Navigating the Doctorate*, focuses on how this population negotiates the professional expectations of graduate study and academia with their personal lives and other obligations.

Peter Mayshle, aka Peter Zaragoza Mayshle, earned his doctorate in English, specializing in rhetoric and composition, from the University of Wisconsin-Madison and his MFA in creative writing (with a focus on fiction) from the University of Michigan. He has taught at Hobart and William Smith Colleges and now teaches at Carnegie Mellon University. His research interests include the rhetorics of space and public memory, ethnography, and postcolonial subjectivities. Mayshle's current book project is called *Walled Memoria: Presencing Memory Sites in Intramuros, Manila,* which investigates the narratives and counternarratives of various memory sites located within the former Spanish colonial center of the Philippines.

Estefany Palacio is a writer and translator, fluent in Spanish and English. She holds a BA in English and recently obtained her MA in professional writing. Throughout her academic career, Palacio has developed an interest in the interaction between digital media and content creation, which is reflected in her outlook on research, writing, and multimedia content development. She holds a creative yet analytical approach to content creation, and, thanks to her background in writing and rhetoric, she has created projects that embrace the use of digital technologies but employ specific rhetorical approaches to ensure a positive user experience.

Lizbett Tinoco is assistant professor of English at Texas A&M University–San Antonio. Her research focuses on writing program administration, community colleges, and multilingualism. She is committed to building equitable and sustainable practices in pedagogy, research, program development, and community engagement.

Kate Vieira is associate professor and the Susan J. Cellmer Distinguished Chair in Literacy in the School of Education at the University of Wisconsin-Madison. She is the author of *American by Paper: How Documents Matter in Immigrant Literacy* (2016; 2017 Honorable Mention CCCC Outstanding Book Award) and *Writing for Love and Money: How Migration Drives Literacy Learning in Transnational Families* (forthcoming). She is a recipient of a Fulbright

Scholar Award (2018–2019), a National Academy of Education/Spencer Postdoctoral Fellowship (2015–2016), a CCCC Research Initiative Grant (2017), and the Donald Murray Prize for Creative Nonfiction (2018).

This book was typeset in Sabon by Barbara Frazier. Typefaces used on the cover include DIN and Blair. The book was printed on 50-lb. White Offset paper by Seaway Printing.

www.ingramcontent.com/pod-product-compliance
Lightning Source LLC
Chambersburg PA
CBHW082102250426
43661CB00078B/2494